To Infinity And Beyond?

The Conundrum Of Delimitation Of Outer Space

Noel Jackson Therattil

Ukiyoto Publishing

All global publishing rights are held by

Ukiyoto Publishing

Published in 2022

Content Copyright © Noel Jackson Therattil
ISBN 9789364940962

All rights reserved.
No part of this publication may be reproduced, transmitted, or stored in a retrieval system, in any form by any means, electronic, mechanical, photocopying, recording or otherwise, without the prior permission of the publisher.

The moral rights of the author have been asserted.

This book is sold subject to the condition that it shall not by way of trade or otherwise, be lent, resold, hired out or otherwise circulated, without the publisher's prior consent, in any form of binding or cover other than that in which it is published.

www.ukiyoto.com

Dedicated to my Parents.

Acknowledgement

My family and friends have been unwaveringly supportive of my efforts through good and bad times. Their support was crucial for the completion of this book and I cannot thank them enough.

My parents have kept me afloat in tough times and given me wings in good times. My mother's unconditional love, unwavering support and belief in me has kept me going through hardships. This book could neither have been conceived nor completed without her.

I would like to thank Ankita especially for helping me with her inputs, feedback, and for constantly cheering me on, all of which have been essential. A good book is after all, the product of dedication and scrutiny.

NALSAR University of Law, Hyderabad
'Justice City', Shameerpet, Medchal-Malkajgiri District - 500 101, Telangana, India.
Tel : +91-40-23498104 / 23498437 Fax : +91-40-23498386
Mobile : +91-99486 60916
E-mail : registrar@nalsar.ac.in, balakista@gmail.com
Website : www.nalsar.ac.in

Prof. (Dr.) V. Balakista Reddy
LL.M., M.Phil., Ph.D. (JNU)
Professor of Law & Registrar

FOREWORD

I have known Noel since he enrolled as a student at the Centre for Aerospace and Defence Laws (CADL). I am delighted to say that this book traces its inception to the first project he was assigned during the pursuance of his Master's degree at CADL. Since then, for the past two years, it had become his passion project which has culminated into this book. It is encouraging to see such an undertaking fructify into an exceptional piece of work.

Over the course of my long career in this field I have found that Space law is deserving of ever more scrutiny. In this day and age, Space Law is no more on the fringe. This book seeks to make the subject of delimitation of Outer Space comprehensible to the lay man, law student and enthusiast alike. It simplifies the verbose language of academic texts while ensuring articulation and brevity. This book makes the subject approachable due to its lucidity. This makes it a must read for those looking to initiate themselves with space law and more specifically, with the subject of delimitation.

It goes beyond the academic commentary of the legal aspects of the delimitation. It ventures into the political, diplomatic, economic and technological determinants of delimitation. The issue is as much political as it is legal and this is given due attention in the book. The book goes on to discuss the various schools of thought and theories proposed in the past 200 years. Finally, he proposes a solution to this conundrum, as it were, which may likely form the basis of delimitation of outer space in the future.

Resolving the issue of delimitation is crucial in addressing present and future concerns of aerospace regulation. It is an issue that a globalizing world needs to address with increasing urgency. National sovereignty, national security, commerce, navigation are just some of the aspects that need to be considered while the international community arrives at a mutual consensus, if at all.

Noel is a person of insatiable curiosity, a quality that I am certain will lead him to undertake new endeavors, and contribute to the growth of legal literature. I wish him the best and hope that this book expands our knowledge and contributes to the richness of our discourse.

Prof. (Dr.) V. Balakista Reddy
Professor of Law and Registrar,
Director, Centre for Aerospace and Defence Laws (CADL),
National Academy of Legal Studies and Research, Hyderabad.

Author's Note

As this book goes to press, we are taking our first steps to becoming an interplanetary species. Near space is no more the final frontier. History is being made, 'giant leaps' are a monthly affair, and competition is rife. Yet, this book contends that we are putting the horse before the cart. We wish to colonize space yet we elect to not define our own domestic boundaries glazed with a potpourri of legal ambiguities.

The question of 'where the sky ends and the heavens begin?' for most of us would appear as a 'no-brainer' culminating in a quick google search. Yet in some corner curiosity remains unsatiated. Where does the firmament lie? This question is one to which we as a species will script the answer. As in Plato's allegory of the cave we must also discover the fire and contemplate the true nature of our world in the 21st century. It is more than a question. It is a test of our cooperation as a community of nation and as a species.

This book seeks to provoke the mind of not just the lawyer and the academician but especially of the layman. Law is the subject of the governed, it's knowledge must be ubiquitous.

Contents

Introduction: The Conundrum	1
Necessity, Challenges And Limits Of State Sovereignty	**4**
Legal position of outer space	4
Considerations and necessity for delimitation	8
Tragedy of the commons.	16
Exploring the limits of State Sovereignty	21
Proposed Methods Of Delimitation	**31**
Methods of Delimitation	31
Novel Methods Suggested for Delimitation	45
Expectations From An Agreeable Methodology	**51**
Considerations Involved	51
Delimitation Policy of States	58
Functionalists And Spatialists	**63**
Theories of delimitation	63
Functionalist Theory	66
Spatialist theory	75
Issues plaguing the spatialist school	79
Resolving The Functionalist And Spacialist Conflict	**83**
Harmonious Construction.	83
Resolving the conflict	90
Role of the ICAO	99

Discovering Neutralia   106

Shared Commonalities with maritime Law and establishment
of Neutralia.   106
Magna Carta of Space   119
Suggested methodology of delimitation.   123

Seeking Delimitation   131

About the Author   146

Introduction: The Conundrum

"Two things fill my mind with ever increasing wonder and awe the more often and the more intensely the reflection wells on them: the starry heavens above me and the moral law within me."

-Immanuel Kant, *Critique of Pure Reason*

In the 117 years since the invention of the first aircraft, humankind has launched objects into outer space and interstellar space. It has placed humans on the Moon and is now primed to step foot on Mars. One might reasonably assume that such scientific achievements would have been accompanied by an appropriate legal framework. Yet, despite the existence of a handful of treaties, principles and declarations, a great deal remains to be covered within a legal framework. The most immediate concern, however, is the need to delineate Airspace and Outer Space.

The need to define a seemingly prosaic concept arises from the practical implications arising from the lack of such delimitation. Consequently, this discourse has been influenced not merely from the legal, scientific, economic and regulatory standpoint but also from the perspective of States zealous of their sovereignty in an increasingly 'global world'.

Space law *per se* may be considered as the collective literature contained in the Treaty on Principles Governing the Activities of States in the Exploration and Use of Outer Space, including the Moon and Other Celestial Bodies (Outer Space Treaty), Agreement on the Rescue of Astronauts, the Return of Astronauts and the Return of Objects Launched into Outer Space (Rescue Agreement), Convention on International Liability for Damage Caused by Space Objects (Liability Convention), Convention on Registration of Objects Launched into Outer Space (Registration Convention), and the Agreement Governing the Activities of States on the Moon and Other Celestial Bodies (Moon Agreement). Yet despite being largely codified, curiously enough, none of the treaties define "Space". This is an outstanding omission considering that most conventions and statues directly or indirectly lay down the limits of the application of the said convention or statute.

However, it must also be kept in mind that at the time the first treaty came into force in October 1967 'space' had largely been the domain of two superpowers, The United States and the Union of Soviet Socialist Republics (USSR). Therefore, the urgency to delimit air and space would have been nonexistent. However, in recent times proliferation of various space agencies and private entities keen on using space has reinvigorated the need to define 'space' for legal, economic, financial and regulatory purposes.

The need for delimiting these two spaces arises primarily from the principles of laws governing these two spaces. It suffices to say that legal frameworks did not account for scientific developments or facts. Nevertheless, laws are fictions made by men that must continuously evolve to stay relevant. As the tides churn so must the law evolve.

The need for a legal regime has gained significance in recent times due to advancements in science. As aircrafts fly higher than ever before, and as satellites orbit closer to the earth a zone where these two objects coexist is steadily evolving. It must also be noted that space crafts have to cross airspace to reach outer space. Numerous permutations and combinations exist before us. Whether the international community must consider some vehicles as aerospace object, aircrafts, or space objects, and whether they would be subject to either air law or space law is a question that rests upon us answering a simple question of 'where does Outer Space begin?'.

Necessity, Challenges And Limits Of State Sovereignty

Legal position of outer space

Land, sea, air and space are the four dimensions of human activity respectively. Delimiting the spheres of land, sea and air is often easy due to the medium in which such activity occurs. Nevertheless, legal fictions do exist in these dimensions so as to create a more acceptable legal framework that respects state sovereignty and allows qualified and unqualified freedom of movement. An example of such legal fiction is exemplified in

Article 1 and Article 2 of the Chicago Convention.[1]

Article 1: *"The contracting States recognize that every State has complete and exclusive sovereignty over the airspace above its territory."*

Article 2: *"For the purposes of this Convention the territory of a State shall be deemed to be the land areas and territorial*

---

[1] International Civil Aviation Organization (ICAO), *Convention on Civil Aviation ("Chicago Convention")*, 7 December 1944, (1994) 15 U.N.T.S. 295

waters adjacent thereto under the sovereignty, suzerainty, protection or mandate of such State"

Similarly, Article 2(2) of the United Nations Convention on the Law of Seas (UNCLOS)[2]. states:

"2. This sovereignty extends to the air space over the territorial sea as well as to its bed and subsoil."

However, the vertical limit of the airspace is not defined or limited. This is in line with the principle of *"Cuius est solum, eius est usque ad coelum et ad inferos."* It translates to "whoever's is the soil, it is theirs all the way to Heaven and all the way to Hell". It extends sovereignty of a state to the skies above it and the Earth under it. In private law it extends the ownership of land rights of a private individual to the sky above his plot.

This is in contrast to Article 1, and Article 2 of the Outer Space Treaty[3] (OST) which states:

Article 1: *"The exploration and use of outer space, including the Moon and other celestial bodies, shall be carried out for the benefit and in the interests of all countries, irrespective of their degree of economic or scientific development, and shall be the province of all mankind. Outer space, including the Moon and other celestial bodies, shall be free for exploration and use by all*

---

[2] United Nations Convention on the Law of the Sea, art 2, Dec. 2, 1982, 1833 U.N.T.S.397 (entered into force Nov. 16, 1994)
[3] Treaty on Principles Governing the activities of States in the exploration and Use of Outer Space, including the Moon and Other Celestial Bodies, 19 December 1966, 610 U.N.T.S. 205 (entered into force in October 1967).

States without discrimination of any kind, on a basis of equality and in accordance with international law, and there shall be free access to all areas of celestial bodies. There shall be freedom of scientific investigation in outer space, including the Moon and other celestial bodies, and States shall facilitate and encourage international cooperation in such investigation."

Article 2: *"Outer space, including the Moon and other celestial bodies, is not subject to national appropriation by claim of sovereignty, by means of use or occupation, or by any other means."*

A harmonious interpretation of articles of UNCLOS and OST highlights that State sovereignty that is applicable to land, sea and airspace is not applicable to outer space and beyond. For this reason, space is often treated at par with the High Seas and Antarctica as it is *Res Communis* or *Res publicae*. Black's Law dictionary defines *Res Communis* as "Things common to all; Things that cannot be owned or appropriated."[4]

This however raises more questions and it answers. The most apparent question it raises is 'where does airspace end and space begin and by implication where does State sovereignty in the vertical plane end?' What complicates it further is that fact that there does not exist any internationally accepted definition of the upper limit of airspace. While some states have claimed an undefined yet limited airspace other states have in some cases claimed an infinite

---

[4] Black's Law Dictionary 1499 (9th ed. 2009).

airspace in the vertical plane. The implications of these definitions will be dealt with later on in the paper.

The next question it raises is as to which legal regime space crafts and aircrafts are subject to. There does not exist any internationally accepted mode to determine as to which legal regime shall apply. However, this issue has numerous ramifications. Determining the violation of airspace, claims of liability in airspace and outer space and determining jurisdiction over an object are among the many issues that would require the adoption of an international accepted legal regime to determine jurisdiction.

Considerations and necessity for delimitation

'Near Space' as we know it is no more the final frontier. Like with all of human history the frontier has been pushed farther away. Every aspect of law requires the establishment of jurisdiction for the effective enforcement of a law. Delimitation allows for the establishment of jurisdiction which in turn permits the creation of a zone of sovereignty or to a limited extent, clarification on the nature of sovereign powers exercisable or not exercisable. The need for jurisdiction becomes particularly important when the uncertainty over jurisdiction is not just within the limits of a sovereign, that is, is not merely municipal. Where the dispute arises between two or more sovereigns there arises a pressing need for a framework based on law, precedent or custom to establish a means for ascertaining jurisdiction or even jurisdictions. The international community until recently was largely apathetic to the need for ascertaining jurisdiction of acts in space. This largely stemmed for the fact that astronauts and spacecrafts were agents and objects of the sovereign respectively. Hence, matters were resolved bilaterally or multilaterally between sovereign states. There are often unwritten understandings in this kind of diplomatic framework. However, with the proliferation of private entities there has arisen a need to extend civil and criminal laws of a state beyond the surface and near surface of Earth and into outer space. The sensitive nature of outer space, its geostrategic and economic importance for national security, and the *sui generis* position of most things associated with outer space, including outer space itself, has led to a further complication in the establishment of jurisdiction.

For a start, addressing this issue of jurisdiction first requires mutual consensus among the international community on the physical delineation of airspace and outer space. It is contingent upon this delineation that a notion of state sovereignty, its extent, and nature can be determined up to and beyond such a physical delineation. A case in point to understand the factors that spawn the need for delimitation is the evolution of maritime delimitation. It is a quintessential example. A perusal of maritime boundaries that have been established shows that these boundaries are more often than not a product of political factors. There is also often an overlap between other factors such as geographical factors with political factors in the delimitation of boundaries. States rarely, if ever, make public the political reasons behind the conclusion of their agreements, which are at times unrelated to the delimitation as such.[5] What this highlights is two important aspects. Firstly, delimitation of outer space and airspace requires more than just a scientific solution. It requires the navigating political sensitivities, addressing questions of national security, territorial sovereignty, and factoring in a State's beneficial and handicap characteristics. A particularly useful example of this characteristic may be the unique claim of certain states upon geostationary orbits via the Bogota Declaration[6]. Secondly and perhaps primordially, delimitation is necessitated by the need to address these concerns in a manner that can withstand the test of time and scrutiny of established legal practice.

The need for addressing political considerations has been acknowledged by the International Court of Justice (ICJ) in the "Continental Shelf (Libyan Arab Jamahiriya/Malta) case.[7] Here the ICJ held that security considerations were "not unrelated to the concept of the continental shelf".[8] A similar concern was raised in the Guinea/Guinea-Bissau case.

Other important grounds for consideration are the safety of sovereign skies. Space has now become a busy hub for both commerce and science. Until recently, capital and technological handicaps had been

---

[5] *Handbook on the Delimitation of Maritime Boundaries*. New York: United Nations Publication, 2000 p.42.
[6] The 1976 Declaration of the First Meeting of Equatorial Countries, Dec 3, 1976
[7] Continental Shelf (*Libya v. Malta*), 1985 I.C.J. 13
[8] *Supra* note 5, at 44

the biggest barriers in realizing the full potential of outer space. However, costs have significantly been reduced in light of technological advancements such as reusable rockets, and the first steps towards full commercialization of space has begun. The cost of launching a Low Earth Object (LEO) into space cost $54,000 per Kilogram, however, innovations made by Space X allow the launch of a LEO at a cost of $2720 per Kilogram (launched using Falcon 9). Similarly, the cost of launching a payload to the International Space Station (ISS) has been reduced by four times from $93,400 per kilogram to, $23,300 per kilogram. [9] Another case in point is Elon Musk's Star Link system, as it would potentially bring in a new 'space and telecommunications' revolution and with it a distinct set of legal challenges.

While on average commercial airliners fly up to a height of 10Km (32,000 Ft), military aircrafts can reach up to 15 Km (50,000 Ft). In 1973, a modified soviet Mig-25 reached an altitude of 36.2 Km. In a span of 4 years this record was broken as another modified Mig-25 reached an altitude of 37.65 Km. In 2004 SpaceShipOne reached the 100Km mark and completed sub-orbital flights. [10] Furthermore, as aircrafts fly higher, space crafts can, and have orbited lower. In 1997, the Soviet Elektron-4 satellite (SSN 748) made 10 revolutions around the Earth at a

---

[9] Harry W. Jones, *The recent large reduction in space launch cost*, in 48th International Conference on Environmental Systems 1 (2018).
[10] International Civil Aviation Organization, *Commercial Space Flights*, (ICAO, Working Paper LC/36-WP/3-2 20/10/15)

perigee of 85Km or below during reentry.[11] Therefore as 'near space' or high-altitude airspace is getting crowded by both space crafts and aircrafts, the probability of collisions between spacecraft and aircrafts increases. It also goes without saying that as the number of average launches annually increases the issue further exacerbates over time. In fact, the number of space launches has been nearly doubling every year.[12]

The issue of ascertaining the applicable legal regime goes beyond the nationality of the personnel. It requires either ascertaining the nature of the object or the position of the object, or both. The necessity to delineate airspace and outer also stem from identifying the nature of liability, the status of the 'personnel' *vis-à-vis* international law, the Geneva Convention and the Rescue convention and most importantly the exercise of state sovereignty. While these were persistent concerns ever since the first space launch the intensity has now increased at a pace that may see states struggling to ensure safe skies.

---

[11] Jonathan C. McDowell, *The edge of space: Revisiting the Karman Line*, 151 Acta Astronautica 668-675 (2018).

[12] Jeff Matthews, The Decline of Commercial Space Launch Costs – Insights to Action | Deloitte US Deloitte United States (2022), https://www2.deloitte.com/us/en/pages/public-sector/articles/commercial-space-launch-cost.html (last visited Apr 13, 2022).

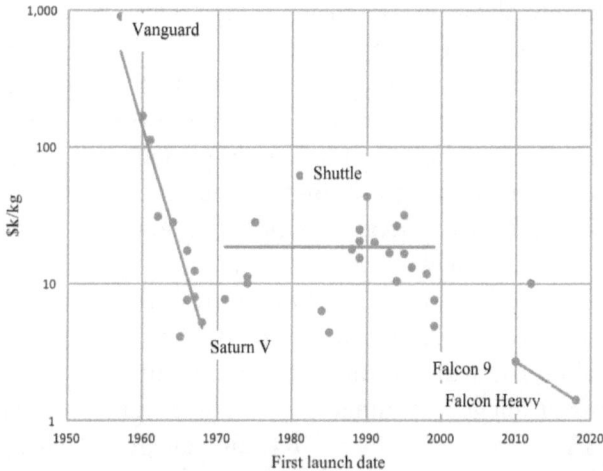

Figure 1: Date of launch and cost per kilogram for launch.[13]

This also prompts a discussion on adressing the need for an integrated regime or a unified regime to govern air space after factoring in outer space and vice versa. The differences are significant if not merely immense. It is patently clear on perusal[14] that merely crossing a line in a matter of seconds can be akin to crossing over from well regulated air space to the 'high seas' of outer space, or as some may call it, the wildwest of outer space.

---

[13] *Supra* note 9, at 2

[14] Paul Stephen Dempsey & Maria Manoli, *Suborbital Flights and the Delimitation of Air Space Vis-À-Vis Outer Space: Functionalism, Spatialism and State Sovereignty*, VOL XLII ANNALS OF AIR AND SPACE LAW 202-206 (2017), https://ssrn.com/abstract=3241421 (last visited Apr 13, 2022).

Commercialization of space brings with it disputes and necessitates legal redressal. Consequently, application of law requires ascertaining appropriate jurisdiction. For instance, as mentioned above, increased launches coupled with growing air traffic also increases the probability of collisions between space crafts and aircrafts while the applicable legal framework remains unclear.

The lack of clear establishment of jurisdiction also extends to the realm of criminal law, to an extent revealing the wide ambit that remains uncovered. The first ever alleged criminal case occurred in 2019 when NASA astronaut Anne McClain allegedly illegally accessed her spouses bank account from a computer onboard the International Space Station (ISS).[15] This case was however straight forward due to procedure established for crimes committed onboard the ISS. Here it is also relevant to note that where the criminal act is committed against a person of the same nationality, active jurisdiction of the state would apply. Where a crime is committed against a personal of another nationality establishing jurisdiction would be more complicated. Passive jurisdiction is most likely to be applicable.[16] Furthermore, the "impact

---

[15] The New Indian Express, *NASA astronaut Anne McClain says she did not hack her spouse's data*, 2019, https://www.newindianexpress.com/world/2019/aug/25/nasa-astronaut-anne-mcclain-says-she-did-not-hack-her-spouses-data-2024085.html (last visited Apr 13, 2022).

[16] Danielle Ireland-Piper, NASA is facing its first space crime — so, what happens if you commit a crime in space? The Print

territoriality" principle can be invoked. It states that a state may prosecute an individual regardless of nationality or location where the crime was committed if it adversely affects the citizens, the State, or the property within such State.[17] An important aspect to note is that States "have been traditionally free to determine their criminal competence and relatively few limitations seem to have been imposed by international law."[18] Importantly, it may be relevant to note here that States have also claimed jurisdiction on the basis of State of embarkations and disembarkation when a crime is committed aboard an aircraft flying above the high seas.[19] While Article VIII of the Outer Space treaty to a limited extent seeks to establish jurisdiction, the ambiguous and almost Delphic wording of the article fails to address substantively the issue of jurisdiction.

In the larger picture, the intergovernmental agreement governing the ISS is an exception to the rule. As it stands, there is no internationally accepted mode of determining jurisdiction.

(2019), https://theprint.in/science/nasa-is-facing-its-first-space-crime-so-what-happens-if-you-commit-a-crime-in-space/284410/ (last visited Apr 13, 2022).

[17] Stephen Gorove, Criminal Jurisdiction in Outer Space, 6 INT'l L. 315 (1972)

[18] *Supra* note 17, at 316

[19] *Id.*

Tragedy of the commons

The 'Tragedy of the Commons' is a problem for property that is held in common between
many people. Aristotle formulates this in his 'Politics' as follows: "For that which is common to the greatest number has the least care bestowed upon it. Everyone thinks chiefly of his own, hardly at all of the common interest; and only when he is himself concerned as an individual. For besides other considerations, everybody is more inclined to neglect."[20] The word common here refers to an open access and unregulated resource. Airspace and outer space which remains unregulated and open to all states is one of the few 'commons' we share.

The tragedy of the commons can be lucidly explained with the help of an example. In a particular situation 100 families are grazing goats on common land. Total milk production is maximised with a thousand goats in total. For every family to increase the efficiency of its herd the most logical solution appears to be that

---

[20] Conor McGlynn, *Aristotle's Economic Defence of Private Property*, XXIX The Student Economic Review 1 (2022), https://www.tcd.ie/Economics/assets/pdf/SER/2015/McGlynn,%20Aristotles%20Economic%20Defense%20of%20Private%20Prpoerty.pdf (last visited Apr 13, 2022).

each family would maintain a herd of 10 goats. However, contrary to first appearances the family can increase the size of the herd to increase the efficiency of its own herd. If a family adds an extra goat beyond the 10 initial goats to their own herd, it will reduce total milk production from the field, but will increase their personal quantity of milk produced by that herd. Hence every family will increase the number of goats in the herd to the detriment of the common capacity but to the benefit of its own personal quantity.

The same issue applies to outer space too. Despite being an extremely large area there has been a rampant increase in usage of this space by each nation. As each nation seeks to make use of this common heritage of mankind it chips away at the potential of a common space. A perfect example of this is the Kessler syndrome. Addressing this requires regulation.

The solution proposed by the ecologist Garett Hardin was "mutual coercion, mutually agreed upon". While in his essay he proposed this solution to address the problem of overpopulation, it can be applied to most problems arising out of the 'commons'.[21] It may very well be applied to the realm of geo-space. The tragedy of the commons is that people acting in their own self-interest will ignore the commons, resulting in

---

[21] Garrett Hardin, *The Tragedy of the Commons: The population problem has no technical solution; it requires a fundamental extension in morality.*, 162 Science (1968),
https://www.science.org/doi/10.1126/science.162.3859.1243 (last visited Apr 13, 2022).

worse living circumstances for everyone.[22] Orbits may be thought of as a resource rather than as a trajectory. They are akin to spectrum; renewable yet limited. While outer space itself is quite vast, the rarity of Low earth orbits (LEO), geosynchronous orbits, and geostationary orbits make these orbits highly sought after. The emphasis laid on occupying these orbits by states has led to a proliferation of satellites in a bid to occupy these orbits since appropriation is not permissible. As states do their best to make the most out of the common heritage of mankind, they continue to fuel the Kessler syndrome. Eventually a tipping point shall be reached where a "chain reaction in near-Earth orbit of hypervelocity collisions that will trap humanity on Earth."[23]

Dr. Shackleford provides a general framework to address this. First, there can be no private or public appropriation of the commons. Second, representatives from all nations must manage resources since a common is considered to belong to everyone. Third, all nations must actively share in the benefits acquired from exploitation of the resources from the common heritage region. Fourth, there can be no weaponry or military installations established in the commons. Fifth, the commons should be

---

[22] *Supra* note 20, at 2

[23] Sarah Louise Vollmer, *The Right Stuff in Geospace: Using Mutual Coercion to Avoid an Inevitable Prison for Humanity*, 51 St. Mary's Law Journal 795 (2020),
https://commons.stmarytx.edu/thestmaryslawjournal/vol51/iss3/6 (last visited Apr 13, 2022).

preserved for the benefit of future generations. According to Hardin for a solution to regulate a system to be accepted then such a solution "must either have a negligible effect on the global community's perceived utility of space access or substantially increase that utility."[24] To this extent it is necessary to make a legal regime that increases the utility of space to all nations and at the same time ensures that the common is not affected to the extent that it affects the common good of all to the detriment of another.

Delimitation of airspace and Geo-space, at least in both the practical and theoretical context has occurred in three phases. The first phase of delimitation was private and public rights over suprajacent airspace. This allowed the public use of what was till that point considered an extension of private property by virtue of the principle of *ad coelum et ad infernos*. The second phase of delimitation was between the exercise of sovereignty by nation states over their airspace and respecting the freedom of navigation in international airspace. In the third phase, delimitation occurred between airspace and outer space. These delimitations though not formally recognised has been hazy and received *de facto* recognition at least by some states. The third phase of delimitation even though hazy is acknowledged by the Outer Space Treaty. Following this, the need for greater regulation led to the acceptance of four other

---

[24] *Id.* at 802

treaties. However, these treaties built upon the outer space treaty and did not create a separate regime.[25] Hence, while there is general agreement that some form of mutually acceptable and amicable system of regulation must exist, the real question is whether there is mutual coercion to the extent that the 'commons' is not exploited by individual states to the detriment of the common.

---

[25] *Supra* note 23, at 787

Exploring the limits of State Sovereignty

The Westphalian world order as it exists has seen increasing international law obligations imposed upon States yet despite this the concept of sovereignty does not lose its absolute character as a result of any international law obligations. "Even the extensive decision-making powers of international courts and arbitral panels cannot eliminate it."[26] The Westphalian notion of State sovereignty has been consistently been reaffirmed by international courts and arbitral panels.

While the limits of state sovereignty in the horizontal plane, that is, land and sea, are well recognized and delimited. The limits of state sovereignty in the vertical plane is recognized but the extent is unclear. The extension of state sovereignty can be traced back to the Latin maxim *"Cuius est solum, eius est usque ad coelum et ad inferos"*; "whoever's is the soil, it is theirs all the way to Heaven and all the way to Hell". The maxim was first cited in the case of Bury v. Pope.[27] The right to airspace above the territory of a state was consequently recognized in the Paris Convention of

---

[26] Hermann Heller & David Dyzenhaus, *Sovereignty: A Contribution to the Theory of Public and International Law*, 173 (Oxford Scholarship Online 2019)

[27] *Bury V. Pope* [1587] Bro Eliz 118.

1919 [28], The Chicago Convention of 1944 [29], and UNCLOS.[30]

However, firstly, it may be pointed out that no court has explicitly stated that the ownership in the vertical plane extends to an indefinite distance.[31] On the contrary courts have highlighted that a maxim cannot be cited as principles of law but mere "signposts". Fredrick Pollock describes a maxim as "a symbol or vehicle of the law".[32]

Secondly, and more importantly, the Outer Space Treaty allows for the "free exploration and use by all States without discrimination of any kind and free access to all areas of celestial bodies."[33] While Article VI of the treaty states that the responsibility for the activities of government and non-government entities

---

[28] Convention Relating to the Regulation of Aerial Navigation, opened for signature Oct. 13, 1919, 11 L.N.T.S. 173.

[29] International Civil Aviation Organization (ICAO), *Convention on Civil Aviation ("Chicago Convention")*, 7 December 1944, (1994) 15 U.N.T.S. 295

[30] UN General Assembly, *Convention on the Law of the Sea*, 10 December 1982

[31] Lora D. Lashbrook, *Ad Coelum Maxim As Applied to Aviation Law*, 21 Notre Dame Law Review 143,144 (1946), available at: https://scholarship.law.nd.edu/cgi/viewcontent.cgi?referer=&httpsredir=1&article=3889&context=ndlr (last visited Apr 14, 2022).

[32] Yehuda Abramovitch, *Maxim "Cujus Est Solum Ejus Usque Ad Coelum" as Applied in Aviation*, 8 McGill Law Journal 2 (1962), available at: https://lawjournal.mcgill.ca/article/maxim-cujus-est-solum-ejus-usque-ad-coelum-as-applied-in-aviation-the/ (last visited Apr 18, 2022).

[33] *Supra* note 3, Art. 2

shall fall upon the "appropriate state". Therefore, it may be concluded that sovereignty of a state in the vertical plane is limited, albeit undefined in view of the lack of delimitation of airspace and outer space. This limit on state sovereignty, however, is qualified as States may exercise their jurisdiction on certain space crafts and space objects. The jurisdiction exercised by a state on a spacecraft is not unlike those exercised by a state on vessels on the high sea.

On this note, it becomes important to delve into the question of the state's jurisdiction. It is true that Article VI establishes the 'responsibility' of a State to the extent of its own international responsibility. The article does not extend the jurisdiction of the State beyond this realm to the extent of the personal or public responsibility of a private individual. This reasoning too may be concluded only by a stretch and only to the extent that the word responsibility overlaps with jurisdiction. Responsibility may also exist where a State has no jurisdiction. For instance, a State may shoulder the responsibility of cleaning up radioactive contamination without having jurisdiction in the area. A case in point being the Palomares incident. [34] Article VIII of the outer space treaty establishes 'jurisdiction and control' over both personal and objects. By stating that the jurisdiction of the state is 'not affected by their presence in outer

---

[34] Gerry Hadden, Palomares bombs: Spain waits for US to finish nuclear clean-up BBC News (2012),
https://www.bbc.com/news/magazine-18689132 (last visited Apr 30, 2022).

space or on a celestial body' it creates a position similar to that of a state's jurisdiction on a vessel on the high seas. At first glance this provision appears to have addressed most concerns but a perusal of past maritime jurisdictional cases belies this conclusion. For instance, Article VIII does not address the jurisdictional competence of a second or third party. Must it be interpreted as a supplement to existing theories of jurisdiction or be considered as a *sui generis* legal framework independent of existing notions of state sovereignty? The Lotus case may be cited as an example of establishing jurisdiction in light of an unclear jurisdictional framework. In that case the court held that "the principle of exclusivity of the flag State, in applying only to acts of authority, is not an obstacle to the jurisdictional competence of foreign tribunals."[35] This position existed till the entry into force of the United Nations Convention of the Law of the Seas (UNCLOS) Article 97 which clarified the position.

In the beginning of the 20th century the rationale for extending state sovereignty to the air space above was the right of 'self-preservation'. In 1902, Paul Fauchille the then Rapporteur for the Institute of International Law on the subject of the legal status of the airships

---

[35] Anne Bardin, *Coastal State's Jurisdiction over Foreign Vessels*, 14 Pace International Law Review 45 (2002), available at: https://digitalcommons.pace.edu/cgi/viewcontent.cgi?referer=&httpsredir=1&article=1188&context=pilr (last visited Apr 18, 2022).

suggested that state sovereignty extended to 1,500 meters from the surface so as to ensure that the state can enforce certain laws and prevent threats to its national security. These threats were described as prevention of espionage, customs and defence among other things.[36] Even though there were objection initially, State later acknowledged and agreed upon extending State sovereignty at the first diplomatic conference to consider flight regulation at Paris in 1910.[37] At the Chicago conference the signing of the Chicago convention acknowledged the right of a State to the airspace above it.[38] The convention does not mention where air space ends but a simple isolated reading of Article 1 gives the impression that it extends without limit subject to it being airspace and not outer space. An even narrower interpretation would mean that State sovereignty extends to all of the space above the territory of the said state. As to what constitutes airspace and consequently establishing the limits of a State sovereignty is a hazy concept. It is not defined by a physical boundary (like with some territorial boundaries such as those that use rivers or watershed as a means of delimitation) or a strict limitation based on distance such as with maritime delimitations. It is instead based upon the

---

[36] Dean N. Reinhardt, *The Vertical Limit of State Sovereignty*, 72 Journal of Air Law and Commerce 70 (2007), available at: https://scholar.smu.edu/cgi/viewcontent.cgi?article=1126&context=jalc (last visited Apr 18, 2022).

[37] *Id.*, at 71

[38] *Supra* note 1, Art. 1

maximum altitude achievable by an aircraft as defined in annex 7 of the Chicago Convention. This theory of delimitation is also referred to as the Logical-Juridical Interpretation or the Aerodynamic lift theory.

In contrast to this, two other notable theories were proposed. The first was Prof. J.C. Cooper's Control theory. Initially he suggested that the limit of State sovereignty be unlimited but upon facing criticism he revised it to state that State sovereignty should extend up to limits stated by the Logical-Juridical Interpretation but beyond that limit extend the State's sovereignty up to 300 miles. The area between the maximum altitude of an aircraft and 300 miles above the surface maybe called the 'contiguous zone' and shall allow passage of only non-military transit flights while ascending or descending. Beyond the said 300 miles all space would be available to all types of flights. [39] Cooper's theory is akin to the existing maritime delimitations. It must be noted here that considering that a major power like the United States has not ratified the UNCLOS and continues to challenge states to reaffirm its own interpretation of international law[40] [41] it may be untenable to such a state to accept a similar delimitation in Air Space.

---

[39] Abdurrasyid Dr. H. Priya, *State Sovereignty in Airspace*, 6 Neliti 487 (2009),
https://media.neliti.com/media/publications/39223-EN-state-sovereignity-in-airspace.pdf (last visited Apr 18, 2022).

[40] Ministry of External Affairs, Government of India, Passage of USS John Paul Jones through India's EEZ (2021), available at: https://www.mea.gov.in/press-

There is also the current consensus, which according to Dr. Gbenga Oduntan, is of the view that there is no need to explicitly discuss and hence attempt to limit the State's right to sovereignty over the air space above it. According to him this theory, called the "No present need theory" is unsatisfactory and would lead to a situation where rights and duties have been delineated but their operational jurisdiction is not delineated hence resulting in rights and duties that are effectively unenforceable.[42] There are numerous other theories that have been suggested and that will be discussed in later chapters. However, it suffices to say that extending State sovereignty and consequently jurisdiction to the farthest point is the primary consensus of most States whether it is acknowledged or not. It stems from the need for self-preservation and economic interests that accompany this sovereignty.

Hence, the international community faces the dilemma of curbing its own sovereignty in order to ensure a predictable legal and political order to evolve and persist. The importance of predictability and

---

releases.htm?dtl/33787/Passage_of_USS_John_Paul_Jones_through_Indias_EEZ (last visited Apr 30, 2022).

[41] U.S. 7th Fleet Public Affairs, 7th Fleet conducts Freedom of Navigation Operation (2021), available at: 7th Fleet conducts Freedom of Navigation Operation > Commander, U.S. 7th Fleet > Display (navy.mil) (last visited Apr 30, 2022).

[42] Gbenga Oduntan, Air Law & Space Law: spatial delimitation between airspace & outer space (2016), https://www.youtube.com/watch?v=QQbHvIj9isA (last visited Apr 18, 2022).

knowability of the legal position is important in the context of promoting the full and fair utilization of outer space. According to Prof. Dr. Ram Jhaku in practice states are going to be guided by economics and politics, predominant among which would be politics. According to him the necessity of commerce and safety will largely dictate the evolution of the space regime especially in near space rather than outer space. Furthermore, according to him it is this unique need that would most likely make ICAO an appropriate body to address this matter and *via* which states can ensure safety above their skies via an international organization. Other organizations such as the International telecommunications Union and United Nations Committee on Outer Space (UNCOPOUS) can also play an important role, greater than they do presently. The ICAO's Worldwide Air Transport Conference's sixth meeting has noted that while "National sovereignty cannot be delegated. But the responsibility for the performance of functional responsibilities, such as the provision of air navigation services, can be delegated to third parties. States retain complete freedom to designate a third-party service provider, be it a national or foreign entity."[43] It further contended that "Delegation to a foreign organisation is not an abandonment of sovereignty; sovereign competences are not impacted.

---

[43] Airspace Sovereignty, *in* Worldwide Air Transport Conference (ATCONF) 2 (2022), http://www.icao.int/meetings/atconf6 (last visited Apr 18, 2022).

On the contrary, delegation of service provision is an act of sovereignty."[44]

It is also due to this existing position that as it stands, a mélange of regulations has been applied to near space and airspace by both international and national organizations.[45] According to Steven Freeland, States believe that a multilateral regulation is required but a push would be required from civil society. According to him the issue "requires a championing".

This indicates the need for broader discussion for ascertaining the extent of state sovereignty despite the fact it will be spurned by domestic needs.[46] However, it is fair to be seen whether states like the United States, Russia, European Union and China will part with the influence that they possess and the *de facto* power they exercise at a time when outer space is largely unregulated and at the mercy of consensus among major powers. This becomes a plausible outcome considering that these gains have been hard won and also because it may be agreed that leading research and innovation has been a product of only a few States. Subjecting these gains to the views of the larger international community would be perceived as 'patently unfair' by major space exploring nations.

---

[44] *Id.*

[45] The Quest for a Legal Frontier between Airspace and Outer Space, *in* Space Law Webinar #2 (2020), https://iaass.space-safety.org/events/courses/space-law-webinar-2-the-quest-for-a-legal-frontier-between-airspace-and-outer-space/ (last visited Apr 18, 2022).

[46] *Id.*

Moreover, according to Stephan Hobe, the implications of military use of outer space make it particularly improbable that major powers will agree to a regulation that would impinge upon their dual use or military use of outer space.[47] A case in point is the deployment of dual use weapons and transit of hypersonic glide vehicles in outer space. The weaponization of outer space may very well be prevented, however, the militarization of outer space is another matter altogether. The deployment of 'non-lethal' weapons and other logistical equipment in outer space is quite likely an inevitability.

---

[47] *Id.*

Proposed Methods Of Delimitation

Methods of Delimitation

The need for delimitation does exist. Even before there arose a pressing need for it there have been proposals made for the delimitation of Airspace and Outer Space. Among the leading authorities on this matter is Oduntan who has suggested that there are nine contemporary theories.[48] More theories can be identified, however, some share certain foundational similarities.

a) No present need theory: This theory has been suggested by some authors who state that 'international necessities will lead to states agreeing upon a delimitation. The theory presupposes that there is an understanding that territorial sovereignty comes to an end at a point albeit a currently undefined one. Another benefit of this theory is the fact that arriving at a consensus via discussion at the United Nations Committee on the Peaceful Uses of

---

[48] Gbenga Oduntan, Sovereignty and Jurisdiction in Airspace and Outer Space - Legal Criteria for Spatial Delimitation xii (1 ed. 2012).

Outer Space may very well be delayed in part due to states themselves as they remain zealous of their territorial sovereignty. Hence, proponents acknowledge, rightly so, that the issue of delimitation is not merely scientific or legal but very much political. Notably, proponents of the theory also argue that establishing a limit may result in a future bone of contention. This also highlights the consternation that in the future it may become nearly impossible to reduce the agreed upon altitude. [49] Pragmatic considerations may also include the future prospect of extending territorial claims to a higher altitude in the future, due to technological innovations or otherwise, which would otherwise effectively be surrendered. Some states have also expressed the view in the UNCOPOUS that the existing framework has functioned well and that until "there was a demonstrated need and a practical basis" [50] for developing a definition or delimitation of outer space the same should not be undertaken. These states contended that "at present any attempt to define and delimit outer space would be a theoretical exercise that could unintentionally complicate existing activities and that might not be adaptable to

---

[49] *Id.*

[50] Addendum to the Draft Report of Committee on the Peaceful Uses of Outer Space, *in* United Nations General Assembly para 33 (2015),
https://www.unoosa.org/pdf/limited/c2/AC105_C2_L296Add 01E.pdf (last visited Apr 18, 2022).

continuing technological developments."[51] Other states had shared their view that that the delimitation of outer space was a management issue and that the UNCOPOUS "Subcommittee and its Working Group could first concentrate on relevant matters that needed practical solutions, such as suborbital flights or launches from flying objects".[52]

b) The present need school: Its many proponents largely consist of developing countries, *inter alia*, Bangladesh[53], Thailand[54], Tunisia[55], Venezuela[56], Qatar[57]. The reason for this according to Oduntan is that most scholars from developed states

---

[51] Addendum to the Draft Report of Committee on the Peaceful Uses of Outer Space, *in* United Nations General Assembly para 33 (2015),
https://www.unoosa.org/pdf/limited/c2/AC105_C2_L296Add 01E.pdf (last visited Apr 18, 2022).

[52] *Supra* note 51, at 34

[53] UNCOPUOS, Questions on the definition and delimitation of outer space: replies from Member States, U.N Doc A/AC.105/889/Add.5, 2, available at Microsoft Word - 737df2ee-7980-44ac-a5c7-64d1f1e0cc8f_in_for_PDF_printing.doc (unoosa.org) (last visited Apr 30, 2022).

[54] *Supra* note 53, at 3

[55] *Supra* note 53, at 4

[56] UNCOPUOS, Questions on the definition and delimitation of outer space: replies from Member States, U.N Doc A/AC.105/889, 3, available at untitled (unoosa.org) (last visited Apr 30, 2022).

[57] UNCOPUOS, Questions on the definition and delimitation of outer space: replies from Member States, U.N Doc A/AC.105/889/Add.4, 3, available at untitled (unoosa.org) (last visited Apr 30, 2022).

have reflected the views of their respective states. While developed states have benefited from the ambiguity pertaining to the delimitation, developing countries have found that a delimitation would reduce conflicts and introduce certainty.[58] To a certain extent it may also reflect concerns of developing states to secure their rights in outer space and play a role in the evolution of space law without having contributed as significantly as the developed countries.

c)   The aerodynamic lift theory / The Kármán Line: Goedhart states displacement of an aircraft in air space may be expressed as weight which is the sum of aerodynamic lift and centrifugal force. At an altitude of 83 km buoyancy of air is not sufficient to sustain the flight of an aircraft. The only method for an aircraft to stay in flight is by the use of Kepler force, which would require the circular velocity of nearly 7,900 m/s. This would effectively make the aircraft a space craft. It is this theory that forms the foundation of the Karman Line. It sets a pragmatic limitation at least upon the flight of an aircraft and bases itself on scientific principles. At first glance it appears to be a methodology based upon rationale principles however it fails to factor in legal, political and military considerations. A state may presently or in the future be in a position to exercise its sovereignty higher up in the atmosphere. Furthermore, keeping in mind the inevitable

---

[58] *Supra* note 48, at 286

technological evolution of crafts, aircrafts and space-based planes could become common. Hence, delimitation based on aerodynamic lift would become redundant. Importantly this theory is a specialization of the spatialist theory and hence would fail to cover space object transiting through the airspace and aircrafts that may transit through outer space. Where the boundary of air space is to be considered as a region to mark delimitation of air space, without regard for aerodynamic lift, the frontier region of Earth's atmosphere known as the Exosphere existing between an altitude of 300 kilometer to 500 Kilometers may be considered. This particular interpretation may do well if nations prefer a strict interpretation of airspace and consequently national airspace. However, according to Bin Cheng the twilight zone at 200 kilometers from the surface of the earth provides a feasible point of delimitation.[59]

d) The 'Special Territorial Jurisdiction' theory / Bogota Declaration theory: States party to the Bogota Declaration lie upon the equator and hence due to their unique geographical position vis-à-vis the geostationary orbit (GSO) lies perpendicularly above them. So as to claim this orbit which is effectively a scarce resource, these states have declared a distance up to 36,000 km from the surface to be within their territorial jurisdiction. A geostationary orbit is different from a geosynchronous orbit due to the fact

---

[59] Bin Cheng, Part I, *From Air Law to Space Law*, *in* Studies in International Space Law 3 (Oxford Scholarship Online 2012).

that it rests on the same plane as that of the equator. Hence, merely three satellites may be enough to cover nearly the whole of the Earth's surface. Members of the Bogota declaration seek to preserve their rights or rather establish rights on this orbit especially considering that most of them are not space faring nations and have not extensively participated in outer space endeavors. According to Gangale, the declaration "lends credence to the idea that certain powerful States had failed to heed the warning expressed in such documents as the ITU Malaga–Torremolinos Convention of 1973, which stipulates inter alia: "Members shall bear in mind that radio frequencies and the geostationary satellite orbit are limited natural resources, that they must be used efficiently and economically."" Furthermore, he states that the use and equitable distribution of these resources have largely been dictated by present and past capabilities of these States and not by the "future competence or capabilities" of developing nations.

e) The functionalist approach/Mission intent line: Some scholars have suggested that instead of being bogged down by the need to establish a spatial delimitation so as to establish jurisdiction a functionalist approach may be adopted. This approach according to its proponents will establish the laws pertaining to outer space to the function of the object or to the point of inception of a space activity. Hence a space shuttle transiting through airspace will be subject to the relevant outer space law and not air space law. Doing so brings clarity to the applicable law and bypasses various concerns. It also finds precedent in the Rescue convention, Liability Convention and Registration convention. However, there are accompanying challenges. These include among other considerations, firstly, states would still like to establish boundaries for the purposes of defense and national security. Secondly, certain rights may become precarious, in particular the right to innocent passage above the territory of a states. Thirdly in instances which requires the application of both legal regimes, such as during a collision or violation of flying rights above a second state, the application of a functionalist theory may further complicate the matter. Furthermore, the question arises whether the spatialist perspective can be completely abandoned. Not only would this require a substantial number of countries to amend their own laws and policies but will also raise concerns pertaining to the enforcement of the Outer Space Treaty and the Moon Treaty. Nevertheless, the functionalist approach has the benefit of being "most reflected in treaty language."[60]

f) The *usque ad infinitum* theory: The proponents of this theory are zealous advocates of State sovereignty. They hold the view that the sovereignty of the State, as mentioned above, stems from the latin maxim and principle of *"Cujus est solum ejus usque ad coelum et ad inferos"*. The value placed upon the

---

[60] Thomas Gangale, How high the sky? The Definition and Delimitation of Outer Space and Territorial Airspace in International Law 92 (2018).

importance of State sovereignty trumps scientific facts or rather, chooses to ignore them when convenient. According to this theory one could argue that momentarily, at a given point of time a State could own a portion of a celestial body the position of which may surpass beyond our very own solar system, at the edge of the universe. In the very next moment the same 'territory' may lie in the sovereign sphere of another state. Furthermore, it ignores the principles enshrined in the Outer Space Treaty and the Moon Treaty that prohibits any State from claiming any part of outer space including celestial bodies as their own. Hence this theory not only fails to acknowledge scientific facts but also fails to consider the position of international law on the subject. Unsurprisingly, this theory has few proponents and even fewer States subscribing to this view.

g) The national security and effective control theory: The foundations of this theory can be found in the origin of the concept of the territorial sea. The width of which was originally based on the distance from the shore which a state could effectively exercise control on. According to this theory the sovereignty of a state shall extend up to the distance it can exercise control especially with regards to the security of the state. *Prima facie* it appears to be a rational view especially considering the importance States lay on their own self-preservation. The fallacy lies in the fact that with the evolution of technology States could theoretically exercise control across vast distance and the literal exercise of control would defeat the purpose of delimitation. Today Anti-Satellite Missile tests (ASAT) are viewed as a means of exercising dominance, if not control, in outer space. However, recognizing the 'region of control' (which may effectively be all of outer space) as the territory of the State may lead to a significant escalation of geopolitical tensions. This theory may get stretched to the point of absurdity. It may hence hinder the implementation of the outer space treaties and particularly the free and unhindered exploration of outer space. Moreover, not all States are in a position to exercise such control. Only a handful of states have such an ability, even among the developed nations of the world. Hence from its very conception the idea may be said to be unfair, undemocratic and impractical. However, Gangale argues that this theory is not necessarily contrary to the spirit of international law. According to him where the effective control theory is tempered by the consideration of legal equality amongst nations then such a theory should be worth of at least consideration. It is also a historic practice of states to establish sovereignty by effective control.[61]

h) The lowest point of orbital flight theory: The theory of lowest orbital point appears to be a viable method of delimitation since it attempts to arrive at a method of delimitation based on scientific principles. It has also been adopted by the International Law Association at its meeting in 1968 in Buenos Aires

---

[61] *Id.*, at 91

and has enjoys acceptance among notable scholars.[62] The theory rests itself upon the notion that a satellite requires a certain altitude to orbit the Earth. An altitude lower than the said amount would result in the satellite burning up due to friction on coming in contact with the atmosphere. Despite appearing to be a rational ground, it is neither possible to establish the appropriate altitude despite factoring in an average nor is it feasible to disregard the technological evolution of Aircrafts and Air-Space crafts. Firstly, satellites come in various shapes and forms, they may have various speeds and have varying compositions. All these factors will affect the altitude a satellite can sustain. Secondly, even if the lowest perigee of the satellite can be established, it assumes that the maximum operable height of aviation is stagnant. This is not the case and it is well known that aerospace technology has allowed for flight not only within the atmosphere but has also been conducive for the propagation of sub orbital flight. Hence while this theory may contribute to the emergence of a viable delimitation method it by and of itself is not capable of fulfilling that role.

i) Zonalization: The idea of dividing space into zones may be said to be similar to the division of maritime boundaries. In 1975 professor C. de Jager and G. Reijnen proposed the division of space into zones. Under the proposal the upper boundary of air

---

[62] Oduntan, *Supra* note 48, at 307

space would be between 50-130 kilometres; the lower limit of this zone was based on the maximum height at which atmospheric flight could be sustained, and the upper limit of this zone was based on the lowest perigee. This space was referred to as 'no-man's space'. The underlying rationale being that no space object could sustain continuous flight or motion in this region and hence could not stay there for long. According to the proposers of this demarcation, satellites alone could *via* sustained 'flight' traverse this region and may traverse this region within a few hours. This region can be accessed by rockets and vehicles using rocket propulsion, and is inaccessible to airplanes and balloons. Hence, in their opinion this region of space is unique. It may very well be so; especially due to the fact that this theory rests upon a legal demarcation coupled with a scientific criterion that buttresses such legal demarcation. There is of course the possibility that in the future, if not the near future, mesospace would also be accessible to aircrafts or other crafts that are not rockets and would sustain their flight for a considerable amount of time. However, it must be said that technology would keep evolving and some rationality may be leveraged so as to not drown rationale grounds on the basis of wire drawn ideas.[63]

---

[63] UNCOPUOS, The Question of The Definition And/Of the Delimitation of Outer Space, U.N Doc. A_AC-105_C-2_7_Add-1, 25, available at
https://digitallibrary.un.org/record/741816?ln=en (last visited Apr 30, 2022).

j) Astronaut Badge Line: This line refers to the 80.5 kilometers altitude, upon crossing which, the United States Air Force, National Aeronautics and Space Administration (NASA), and the Federal Aviation Administration (FAA) award the Astronaut Badge.[64] While this is in no way a legal or scientific methodology it implicitly acknowledges the special recognition of the region beyond the 80 Kilometre distance. Moreover, while this methodology is not in itself a ground deserving consideration, the fact that the distance from the surface is nearly the same as the originally proposed distance by Von Karman of 83.8 Kilometres merits consideration. The Federal Aviation Administration has also been considering reducing the boundary of space - for its own purposes – from 100 kilometres to 80 kilometres citing a "compelling scientific case". This includes data/modelling of "latitudinal variations during solar cycles, theoretical lift coefficients for different size/configuration satellites ranging from CubeSats to the International Space Station, perigee/apogee elliptical analysis of actual satellite orbital lifetimes etc)"[65]. It must be noted that despite this the United

---

[64] Alex S. Li, *Ruling Outer Space: Defining the Boundary and Determining Jurisdictional Authority*, 73 Oklahoma Law Review 726 (2021), https://digitalcommons.law.ou.edu/olr/vol73/iss4/4 (last visited May 4, 2022).

[65] Statement about the Karman Line, World Air Sports Federation (2018), https://www.fai.org/news/statement-about-karman-line (last visited May 4, 2022).

States does not recognize this line nor does it support the delimitation of outer space.[66]

k)   Theory of arbitrary distances: The theory of arbitrary distances is as arbitrary as the most farcical of any suggested theory if not more. However, where it does stand out is the fact that it allows States or preferably the international community from establishing a delimitation based not on scientific facts but on the political, socio-economic and security needs of the States. These criteria would make it more appealable to various stakeholders and will be devoid of uncertainty and be immune to technological progress. The theory of arbitrary distances proposed by Oduntan comes under heavy criticism from Gangale, so much so that Gangale describes Oduntan's advocacy of the theory as having "chain-sawed the child (referring to the other theories) in half and then quartered it as well for good measure."[67]

---

[66] *Supra* note 54.
[67] Gangale, *Supra* note 60, at 62

DISTANCES PROPOSED[68]	
Proposer	**Distance (Km)[69]**
Murphy	48 (6437 for neutral states during wartime)
Azreges	200 - 300
Cheng	499-982 (Later revised to 483 – 805)
Danier	1,046
Galina and Meyer	11265
Westlake	327,000 / 161,000 (Based on rational approximations made by accepting 'immunity —from— falling—objects approach'

---

[68] Gbenga Oduntan, *The Never Ending Dispute: Legal Theories on the Spatial Demarcation Boundary Plane between Airspace and Outer Space*, 1 Hertfordshire Law Journal 64, 81 (2003), http://www.herts.ac.uk/fms/documents/schools/law/HLJ_V1 I2_Oduntan.pdf (last visited May 4, 2022).
[69] Distances have been rounded off.

Novel Methods Suggested for Delimitation

The *sui generis* nature of the issue prompted early scholars to propose novel methods of delimitation. Even today these methods may be considered to be a class apart. These proposed methods may have at one time appealed to reason but now are largely redundant in light of pragmatic considerations of the space age. Nevertheless, it is worth mentioning some of these methodologies in the interest of further understanding the issue and the views that these ideas were based upon. The following methodologies are based on the spatialist view. This may be attributed to the fact that at the time space faring objects were few if not nonexistent.

a)   Gravity: It was suggested that since the gravitational force of the earth was largely uniform and the extent to which it had an influence was uniformly limited, the proposed delimitation could be based upon the extent of Earth's gravitational influence. It was John Cooper who in 1951 suggested an altitude of 259,100 kms because at this distance an object which has attained escape velocity would leave Earth's area of attraction and pass into the gravitation control of the sun.[70] However, a few questions remain

---

[70] Gangale, *Supra* note 60, at 64

unanswered; what happens if an object reaches 259,100 Kms in altitude but does not possess the required escape velocity, can the said object be said to have gone into outer space ? Or can it be said to be in airspace merely because it does not possess the required altitude?

This theory developed further, and it was suggested by Kroell that State sovereignty must extend up to the point where this gravitational force was balanced since any point where the said gravity was not balanced could be used to drop weapons onto the State. Kroell's reference to a point where gravity is balanced or neutralized perhaps refers to the Lagrange points which can be formed due to the interaction of the Sun's or Moon's gravity with that of Earth's.

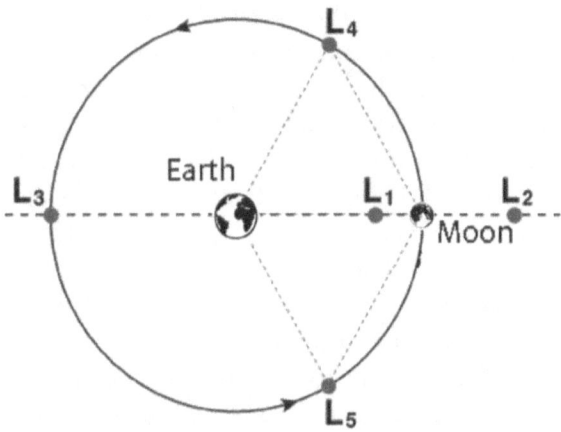

Figure 2: Lagrange points of the Earth and the Moon.

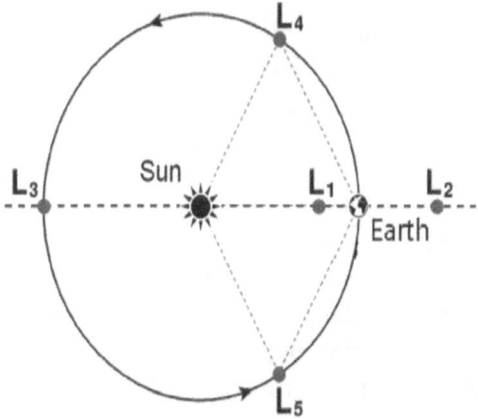

Figure 3: Lagrange points of the Earth and the Sun.

The absurdity of the Kroell's theory becomes apparent on considering a lucid example. Assuming that an object is dropped upon a State from near a Lagrange point formed due to the Sun or the moon, or further away, then the said object can be assumed to be dropped from a distance anywhere between 421,000 Km (Earth Moon L2) or 1.5 million Km (Earth Sun L2). The object even upon reaching its terminal velocity would take a few days to reach its destination by which time the earth would have spun and the target country would be at a different location. Furthermore, the gravitational influence of the earth is theoretically unlimited. The laws of physis clearly state - and it is an evident fact - that gravitational influence has no limit. It continues to extend to infinity and is only weakened by distance. The force of gravity has been represented as $\frac{Gm_1 m_2}{r^2}$ hence Gravity only diminishes by the square of the distance according to this equation of Newton.

b)   Ability to support life: In 1934 Marcel le Goff defined airspace as the layer of the atmosphere where human life is possible. Hubertus Strughold, sometimes called the father of space medicine, wrote of a "biological jurisdictional line" in 1958. According to Strughold, "We face complete biological anoxia at about 16 km. despite free molecular oxygen in the atmosphere up to 90 km…. It is in this narrow zone that the stage for the drama of life on our planet is normally set. Only this layer deserves the name atmosphere, which from the Greek word 'atmos' means 'breath'".[71] While the methodology would have been largely accepted during its time of inception due to the then scientific feasibility and practicality. However, in modern times this does not apply anymore. Oxygen masks and tanks, coupled with pressurised space suits, have meant that humans have been able to sustain life even on the moon to a limited extent. Establishment of human colonies in outer space is a certainty in the foreseeable. Even now, hours long journey in aircrafts are made at altitudes too high to sustain biological life with the exception of perhaps some bacterial life. Another flaw with this theory is that it fails to take into consideration the legal and political issues which are apparent on the face of it.

c)   Relativity: This may come across as the most absurd of methods proposed for the delimitation of outer space. Mateesco Matte relied on "relativistic phenomena such as time dilation due to velocity and the gravitational bending of light, Euclidian and non-Euclidian geometry, Cartesian and Gauss coordinates, the problem of plotting the shortest course between two points on the surface of Earth, and the relativistic effects of the Sun's gravity on the orbit of Mercury"[72] to arrive at the delimitation of outer space on earth. Clearly, as one might imagine, it didn't not result in any easy to deduce method for the delimitation of outer space. On the contrary it only complicated a

---

[71] Gangale, *Supra* note 60, at 104
[72] *Id.*

matter scientifically which was already politically and legally complicated due to competing interests.

Expectations From An Agreeable Methodology

Considerations Involved

In the pursuit of seeking a spatialist demarcation of outer space, we have been unable to arrive at a meaningful delimitation. Nevertheless, as cliché as it may appear, we are now in the possession of what not to rely on as a basis for delimitation. On perusal of all of the methods of delimitation mentioned in the prior chapters, we can reach the conclusion that the following criteria's must be fulfilled for a methodology to be acceptable by the international community.

Firstly, delimitation must take into consideration present scientific and technological capabilities. It must also take into consideration the inevitable development of technology. It is necessary that when a methodology is arrived at, especially one that relies of specialist views, the said methodology must survive the test of technological progress. Like the delimitation of the seas in international law, a methodology must be ubiquitous to all scenarios without exception.

Secondly, delimitation must not be overly complicated. The intention of any delimitation is to mark the boundary between two areas. It is expected that when the international community arrives at a mutually agreeable delimitation, that such delimitation and its methodology is understandable. Again, one may rely of the delimitation of the seas. The process of delimitation may be as simple as agreeing upon a distance. More importantly, the methodology to deal with complex issues such as internal seas are codified in a lucid and simple manner in the United Nations Convention on the Law of the Seas. It may be said that adopting methods or markers that are not easy to distinguish would merely aid in complicating matters. Difficulties would thus arise if, for instance, the earth's atmosphere, the gravitational field or the radiation belt were adopted as a criteria; none of these determinants have visible or clearly discernible frontiers, they would require additional conditionalities.[73]

Thirdly, delimitation must take into consideration political and legal necessities. It is not sufficient that it be based solely upon scientific prerequisites. It may appear counterintuitive to base what appears to be a scientific fact upon man made fictions. As opposed to laws of nature these may be perceived as imaginary or irrational. However, this would not be unprecedent or contrarian since our political and legal consideration

---

[73] Gangale, *Supra* note 60, at 94

are after all fictions we create for an orderly society. Despite this, it is necessary to take scientific realities into consideration. Carl Q. Christol contended that "space must serve the needs of mankind, and that legal rules must be man oriented and must serve human needs."[74] His contention is justified especially since the very concept of outer space is a legal fiction. A scientific view would be that the earth itself is part of outer space, a mere drop in a vast sea. However the human-earth view would be that it is for the benefit of mankind that outer space be governed by that legal fiction and that all methodologies for delimitation also adhere to the sensitivities of legal and political necessities.

As it stands the political divisions on this matter are, as of AD 2022, clear and unambiguous. At the UNCOPOUS's Legal Subcommittee's Sixty-first session the views presented by the delegates could be summarised as:

a) "There was no need to seek a legal definition or delimitation of outer space. The current framework had presented no practical difficulties. An attempt to define or delimit outer space would be an unnecessary theoretical exercise that could unintentionally complicate existing activities and that might not allow

---

[74] Gangale, *Supra* note 60, at 11

for adaptation to continuing technological developments."[75]

b) "Absence of a definition and delimitation of outer space might create legal uncertainty that could affect the application of outer space law and air law, and that the matters concerning State sovereignty over airspace and the scope of application of the legal regimes governing airspace and outer space needed to be clarified to reduce the possibility of disputes among States."[76]

c) "Regulating launches to orbit and suborbital launches, the purpose and function of the mission should be considered. Defining where space began was not necessary to be able to regulate those activities and was not required when considering future space traffic management approaches."[77]

d) "Delimitation of outer space should be considered solely as a definition of the limits of airspace and outer space in terms of the different legal regimes."[78]

e) "Delimitation of outer space was an important topic that should be kept on the agenda of the Legal Subcommittee and that more work should

---

[75] UNCOPUOS, Draft report, U.N Doc. A/AC.105/C.2/L.321/Add.2, 2.

[76] *Id.* at 3.

[77] *Supra* note 75.

[78] UNCOPUOS, Draft report, U.N Doc. A/AC.105/C.2/L.321/Add.2, 2.

be done in that regard, as the legal regimes governing airspace and outer space were different."[79]

Methodologies cannot be to the exclusion of the interests of other nations. The Bogota declaration is a quintessential example of the fact that a treaty that seeks to create an exclusive right will be met with rejection. A method of delimitation that seeks to exclude another nation from access to what the Outer Space Treaty describes as 'the common heritage of mankind' would be to negate the very premise upon which the foundations of international space laws are based. Such a methodology must also take into consideration the technological development across the globe so as to ensure that a lack of technological advancement does not result in a denial of access to outer space, or the enforcement of sovereign rights of a State.

Beyond these requirements it is also necessary for the international community to rationalize its own requirements. For example, the need to protect the territory of a state from security threats in the face of evolving technological improvements cannot be cited as grounds for extending the altitude of delimitation. Doing so would result in outer space in the scientific sense failing to overlap with the legal definition of outer space.

---

[79] *Id.*

Methodology for delimitation must trace its legal grounds ideally to a convention rather than customary law. The rationale being that no precedent exists that can provide a framework for contemporary delimitation of outer space. M. Dauses has also suggested that demarcation of such a boundary must be addressed by an international convention that must be arrived at by the United Nations based on "scientific and legal" considerations. He suggests that a delimitation must be at a distance of 80 Kilometers "from the nearest point of international ellipsoid reference".[80] He defines 'International Ellipsoid of reference' as "ellipsoid of revolution of the earth the semi-major axis of which is 6,318,388 metres and the oblateness of which is 1:291". An obvious limitation with this particular delimitation is that it is convoluted for practical applications. A mere agreement on the same altitude would have sufficed. Nevertheless, the point that a methodology must base itself on a convention and not customary law is a fair conclusion. A delimitation must be well thought out and not base itself on terrestrial customs. New 'spaces' require laws that are *sui generis* to the spaces which it seeks to regulate or govern.

Another obvious issue concerning the adoption of customary law would involve the following questions:

---

[80] UNCOPUOS, The Question of The Definition And/Of the Delimitation of Outer Space, U.N Doc. A_AC-105_C-2_7_Add-1, 26, available at
https://digitallibrary.un.org/record/741816?ln=en (last visited Apr 30, 2022).

a) Whether the said customary law would be flexible enough to accommodate evolving technologies and scientific development while concomitantly ensuring that delimitation of outer space evolves with time and keeps up with technological progress?

b) Whether the said delimitation would adversely affect the national security concerns of States or extend the national security domain to the detriment of technologically disadvantaged states?

c) How would the said delimitation based on customary law would adversely or positively affect the safety of aerospace. This includes not just 'mesospace' but the entirety of outer space.

Delimitation Policy of States

As it stands, there does not appear to be an any existing customary practice that has contributed towards an international consensus on the delimitation of outer space and consequently definition of outer space. In light of this Frans G. von der Dunk suggests that due to the lack of "uniform interpretation, definition and delimitation of outer space" no treaty may be arrived upon however customary law may evolve on consideration of the *opinion juris sive necessitatis* of the various States that have domestically or internationally taken a position on the matter, explicitly or implicitly. According to him the practice of States that have played a special role in the exploration of outer space, and those that occupy an outstanding position in this regard, are of particular importance.[81]

The UNCOPUOS has been leading the effort in reaching an internationally accepted definition of outer space since 1966.[82] Over the past five decades,

---

[81] Frans G. von der Dunk, *THE DELIMITATION OF OUTER SPACE REVISITED The Role of National Space Laws in the Delimitation Issue*, 51 Space, Cyber, and Telecommunications Law Program Faculty Publications 255 (1998), https://digitalcommons.unl.edu/spacelaw/51 (last visited Apr 13, 2022).

[82] U.N.Committee on the Peaceful Uses of Outer Space, *Historical summary on the consideration of the question on the definition and delimitation of outer space*, 3, U.N Doc. A/AC.105/769.

definitions were proposed, however, none were accepted. In 1975, Italy proposed that outer space be delimited at about 90Km. In 1977, some delegations had proposed a height of 90Km to 100Km and one delegate had proposed a "very low limit".[83] In 1978, some delegation had proposed that outer space should be a region between 100Km and 110 Km. Importantly, they added that "that space objects should maintain the right of flight over the territories of States at lower altitudes when they went into orbit or returned to Earth in the territory of the launching State." [84] In 1983, at the 22nd session of UNCOPOUS's Legal Committee the USSR submitted a detailed paper proposing that the delimitation should be at an altitude not more than 110Km.[85]

The most popular although not legally or internationally accepted definition is the Von Karman line which proposed a height of 100Km. There are other numerous definitions that range from a mere 30Km to 1.5 million Km.[86]

The UNCOPOUS had invited member states to submit the position of outer space according to their national legislation and practice relating to definition

---

[83] Lubos Perek, *Scientific Criteria for the Delimitation of Outer Space*, 5 J. Space L. 111 (1977).
[84] *Supra* note 82.
[85] *Id.*
[86] Jonathan C. McDowell, *The edge of space: Revisiting the Karman Line*, 151 Acta Astronautica 668 (2018).

and delimitation of outer space.[87] A few notable ones may be cited.

a) Vietnam's restricted airspace "extends from the surface towards infinity." Further, its 2003 Law on National Borders provides that "the national border in the air is the vertical plane stretching upward from the land border and national border at sea."[88] It may therefore extend to infinity. However, this definition is neither tenable in international law nor desirable.

b) Austria has accepted a definition based on a scientific premise as provided in the Austrian Aviation Rules.[89] It states, "Upper State Boundary — USB: the altitude at which aircraft can no longer move by aerodynamic lift but only according to Kepler's force."[90] However, as technology permits aircrafts to fly higher this definition may be redundant. More importantly, it is not clear whether objects powered by rockets can be considered as aircrafts, as in the case of SpaceShipOne.

---

[87] U.N Office on outer space, Documents and Resolutions Database, https://www.unoosa.org/oosa/documents-and-resolutions/search.jspx?view=&match=A%2FAC.105%2F865 (last visited Apr 13, 2022)

[88] UNCOPUOS, *National legislation and practice relating to the definition and delimitation of outer space*, ,2, U.N Doc A/AC.105/865/Add.23.

[89] Austrian Aviation Rules were revised in 2014 (see Austrian Federal Law Gazette II No. 297/2014)

[90] UNCOPUOS, *National legislation and practice relating to the definition and delimitation of outer space*, 1, A/AC.105/865/Add.19.

c) Belarus has opted for a fixed limit for delimiting outer space. According to the Belarusian Air Code and the Rules for the Use of Airspace, outer space is said to begin at an altitude of 20,100 meters.[91] A fixed height is neither susceptible to a scientific development nor is it untenable in international law.

d) Australia has not defined or delimited outer space but under the Australia's Space Activities Act, 1998, it regulates space activities that occur only above an altitude of 100Km.[92]

e) New Zealand under the Outer Space and High-altitude Activities Act, 2017[93] does not define outer space but defines 'high altitude' as "an altitude above Flight Level 600 (approximately 50Km) and the highest upper limit of controlled airspace under the Civil Aviation Act, 1990"

f) Mexico by virtue of Article 42 of its constitution claims all space above its territory to be its own to "the extent and in accordance with the rules established by international law".

Most member states, however, have neither defined outer space nor do they domestic legislations that seeks to do so. These include, *inter alia,* Australia, Czech Republic, France Mexico, Peru, Turkey and United Kingdom.

---

[91] UNCOPUOS, *National legislation and practice relating to the definition and delimitation of outer space*, A/AC.105/865/Add.4, (February 9, 2009)

[92] *Id.*

[93] Outer Space and High-altitude Activities Act (New Zealand), No. 209 of 2017, 4 (2017).

On perusal of the provisions of The United States' National Aeronautics and Space Act of 1958, according to Frans G. von der Dunk airspace is implied to mean 'within' the atmosphere, while outer space is implied to mean 'outside' the atmosphere and hence "point to a distinct borderline, most probably at some 80 to 100 kms."[94] However, it must be noted that the atmosphere of the Earth according to the National Aeronautics and Space Agency's own website can extend to 10,000 km.[95] Hence, it may not be tenable to assign an altitude by virtue of the Agency's functions.

---

[94] *Supra* note 81, at 257
[95] Brian Dunbar, Earth's Atmospheric Layers NASA (2013), https://www.nasa.gov/mission_pages/sunearth/science/atmosphere-layers2.html (last visited Apr 13, 2022).

Functionalists And Spatialists

Theories of delimitation

The international community on this issue has by and large, been divided into two schools of functionalists and spatialists. These schools have sought to determine the future of human space travel, space colonization, and of course, the exploration of outer space for the greater good of mankind. These theories of delimitation differ on the fundamental premise of the mode of delimitation. To put it succinctly, the difference between the two theories may be lucidly described as establishing jurisdiction on an object based upon its function, or upon the region it traverses through.

Even though states have usually staunchly held on to their positions either in the functionalist or specialist camps ever since the first Scientific and Technical Subcommittee of the Outer Space Committee, some States have changed their views on the matter. Belgium which had remained in the functionalist camp, in 1976 submitted its paper to the subcommittee and suggested a delimitation of outer space at an altitude of 100 kilometres. Famously, even the Soviet Union which was also in the functionalist camp and had even criticized the above-mentioned Belgian suggestion of 100 kilometres as arbitrary, decided to also suggest a similar proposition. This was followed by other Soviet bloc states. [96] While the spatialist view has now become more dominant as compared to the beginning of the space age. Nevertheless, the hesitation surrounding it persists due to the following reasons:

a) Inability of states to monitor a boundary a 100 kilometres perpendicular to the ground: This brings with it logistical challenges. While modern technology now allows for a state to monitor air space to such an extent the question that begets us is what happens in the eventuality of states developing technology to extend and enforce sovereignty up to an altitude extending beyond 100 Kilometres.

b) Lack of examination of other relevant considerations such as political, technical, legal and scientific factors: This methodology cannot be reliant on merely one consideration even if that may be the single most important one. Harmonious synergy between these foundational considerations is essential.

c) Inelastic boundaries that may stifle exploration of outer space in the future: A fixed spatial boundary carries with it the probability of

---

[96] Bin Cheng, Part IV, *The Legal Regime of Airspace and Outer Space: the Boundary Problem Functionalism versus Spatialism: the Major Premises*, *in* Studies in International Space Law 3 (Oxford Scholarship Online 2012).

limiting the scope for exploring outer space for future generations. A fixed boundary established in this day and age would most likely fail to take into consideration the capability of future technologies. More precisely, human nature largely lacks the ability to peer into the scientific prowess of future generations. Hence ascertaining a spatial delimitation that would be flexible or rather, 'accommodative yet rigid' is a challenge in itself.

Functionalist Theory

The functionalist theory states that the legal regime that would be applicable hinges upon the nature of the activity rather than the location where the activity in question occurs.[97] Therefore, the 'orbital' character of the object would determine applicable legal regime.[98] The functionalist perspective by implication rejects the notion that a line based on any criteria or consideration may serve to delimit outer space. This approach has certain benefits. Firstly, the functionalist theory has been incorporated into a number of sub-regimes.[99] *Ergo*, the very sanctity of these regimes rests upon the recognition of the functionalist theory. For instance, the Rescue Convention [100] and Registration Convention [101] are applicable regardless of the location of the object. More often than not

---

[97] UNOOSA Press Release, *The Definition and Delimitation of Outer Space: The Present Need to Determine Where "Space Activities" Begin*, available at: https://www.unoosa.org/pdf/pres/lsc2014/tech-04E.pdf

[98] Proceedings of the Fortieth Colloquium on the Law of Outer Space, *in*40th Colloquium on the Law of Outer Space (1997).

[99] *Supra* note 81, at 225

[100] Agreement on the Rescue of Astronauts, the Return of Astronauts and the Return of Objects Launched into Outer Space, Dec *19 1967, 610 UNTS 205*

[101] Convention on registration of objects launched into outer space, Sep 15, 1976, 1023 UNTS 15

these conventions apply when the object in question is not in outer space, or does not have an orbital trajectory. It may be pointed out that the implied existence and recognition of the functionalist theory is, in part, also responsible for the fact that delimitation of space has not been achieved to this date.[102]

Dr. G. Gal (Hungary), in his paper entitled "30 Years of Functionalism" argues that the prior recognition of the functionalist theory would be a realistic method for delimitation or the lack of it. He further argues that where delimitation was to be done at a certain altitude, the functionalist approach would play a determining factor.[103] It has also been pointed out that a functionalist approach would "permit free access to all areas of outer space and the celestial bodies, because these rights do not necessitate territorial appropriation, national claims of sovereignty."[104] At the UNCOPOUS's Legal Subcommittee's Fifty-fourth session some delegations expressed the view that "in relation to the definition and/or delimitation of outer space, it would be preferable to focus on the function and purpose of an object rather than on its location, in order to

---

[102] *Supra* note 81, at 256
[103] International Institute if Space Law, *The 40th Colloquium on the Law of Outer Space Turin, Italy*, 6, (October 7, 1997) (Available at: http://www.iislweb.org/docs/1997%20IISL%20REPORT%20TURIN.pdf) last accessed on 24-11-2020
[104] *Id.*

determine if and when space law would govern its activities."[105]

The determination of the applicable legal regime especially on an aerospace object that traverses both airspace and outer space is particularly important yet a particularly sticky point of contention. Some states are of the view that for such objects the functionalist view can perhaps help in addressing this quandary. Responding to the 'Questionnaire on Possible Legal Issues with Regard to Aerospace Objects' circulated by the United Nations Committee on The Peaceful Uses of Outer Space some states expressed the view for a functionalist approach to resolving the issue. Some delegations expressed the view that in relation to the definition and/or delimitation of outer space, it would be preferable to focus on the function and purpose of an object rather than on its location, in order to determine if and when space law would govern its activities. [106] The following countries justified the functionalist view.

---

[105] UNCOPUOS, Draft report, U.N Doc. A/AC.105/C.2/L.296/Add.1, 5, available at Microsoft Word - fb25d410-4551-43fe-8305-ccc82316b0d9_in_for_PDF_printing.doc (unoosa.org) (last visited Apr 30, 2022)

[106] Addendum to the Draft Report of Committee on the Peaceful Uses of Outer Space, *in* United Nations General Assembly para 31 (2015), https://www.unoosa.org/pdf/limited/c2/AC105_C2_L296Add 01E.pdf (last visited Apr 18, 2022)

a. Egypt: It submitted that complications in the legal regime applicable to the aerospace object and so as to avoid the 'problems that may arise on applying two regimes', the relevant foreign state must be notified. Furthermore, where the purpose of the object is to conduct a mission in airspace then the object should be subject to air law.[107]

b. Chile: It is of the view that there should be no distinction made with respect to the regime applicable to an aerospace object where the purpose of a mission is a 'space mission' or the destination was in outer space It also advocated for the establishment of provisions pertaining to innocent passage of these objects while traversing through national air space.[108]

c. Greece: It was firmly of the view that the applicable legal regime should not be determined by the *ratione loci* of the object. Instead, the space object must be subject to only one legal regime so as to avoid unnecessary dualism, in part, due to the high speeds at which space objects travel and also to reduce "confusion and malfunction of the whole legal system governing space activities."[109] Therefore, where the purpose of the flight is to conduct outer

---

[107] UNCOPUOS, Questionnaire on possible legal issues with regard to aerospace objects: replies from Member States, U.N Doc. A/AC.105/635/Add.15, 3, available at untitled (unoosa.org) (last visited Apr 30, 2022).

[108] UNCOPUOS, Questionnaire on Possible Legal Issues with Regard to Aerospace Objects: Replies from Member States, U.N Doc. A/AC.105/635/Add.15, 4-5, available at: A_AC.105_635_Add.3-EN.pdf (last visited Apr 30, 2022).

[109] *Id.*

space activities, all the activities of the object including its launch should be subject to space law. However, it must be emphasized that provisions relating to air space safety should be complied with.

d. Türkiye: It has adopted the functionalist view. However, it makes a notable clarification; where the destination consist of both airspace and outer space the applicable regime which the object is subject to should be clearly specified.[110]

e. Nigeria: It is of the view that the functionalist view shall apply. It should be the functionality of the object that determines the applicable regime. The rationale cited by Nigeria is that outer space is a global common and that since no State or person may establish any claim *in rem* the functionalist perspective shall be applicable.[111]

f. United States of America: In the United States while there is no clear adoption of a functionalist or spacialist perspective, the National Aeronautics and Space Act seeks to govern space activities conducted in outer space while drawing a distinction between air space and outer space. Meanwhile, The Satellite Remote Sensing Acts of the United States seeks to

---

[110] UNCOPUOS, Questionnaire on Possible Legal Issues with Regard to Aerospace Objects: Replies from Member States, U.N Doc. A/AC.105/635/Add.14, 5, available at: Microsoft Word - V0780807.doc (unoosa.org) (last visited Apr 30, 2022).

[111] UNCOPUOS, Questionnaire on Possible Legal Issues with Regard to Aerospace Objects: Replies from Member States, U.N Doc. A/AC.105/635/Add.13, 4, available at: https://www.unoosa.org/pdf/reports/ac105/AC105_635Add13E.pdf (last visited May 4, 2022).

establish jurisdiction upon all private entities having substantial connection with the United States. Such jurisdiction hence is applicable regardless of spatial positioning of any connected activity.[112]

Notable states have also created a classification based on functionalism rather than seek delimitation of outer space. Among these are the major space faring nations, including the Russian Federation, The United States, and the United Kingdom. The Russian Federation especially has taken a wide interpretation of the functionalist perspective. It considers space activities to include anything "immediately connected" with the use and exploration of outer space. It also includes within its ambit any "any services necessary for carrying out these activities. It is also worthwhile to point out that Russian jurisdiction covers within its ambit the object and the crew both while in outer space and notably "on return to the earth outside the territorial jurisdiction of the state."[113]

However, despite its limited implied acceptance, at least in the terms of the number of subscribing members, the functionalist approach does have certain shortcomings which have hindered its adoption. While the relevant regime may be determined on the basis of the nature of an object and the activity it performs, the nature of the object or its activity remains undefined and ambiguous.

---

[112] *Supra* note 81, at 258
[113] *Supra* note 81, at 256, 257

What is a 'space craft' and what counts as 'space activity' remains undefined. Annex 7 of the Chicago convention defines an aircraft as "Any machine that can derive support in the atmosphere from the reactions of the air other than the reactions of the air against the earth's surface."[114] It may be noted that the annex also considers balloons and gliders as aircrafts. On the contrary there does not exist any internationally accepted definition of a 'space craft'. The Liability Convention and Registration convention define 'space object' as "space object includes component parts of a space object as well as its launch vehicle and parts thereof." These conventions do not define what constitutes a space craft. The ambiguity has been pervasive. However, at the proceedings of the thirteenth colloquium on the law of outer space (1970) the term Space Object was defined as "a man-made object launched into space beyond atmospheric space" and a space vehicle was simple defined as "a space object carrying equipment and/or persons" by Prof. P. Magno and Dr. E. Scifoni. This definition is perhaps amongst the clearest definitions of a space object however it relies of on a spatialist view and is also outdated since modern technology allows an object to travel beyond atmospheric space but not reach into outer space. An example of this is Space Ship One.

Furthermore, as science has progressed and continues to progress aircrafts are performing certain functions

---

[114] *Supra* note 1, Annex 7

of a space craft. Aircrafts that will attempt to gain suborbital flight for space tourism would be performing activities pertaining to space travel for a limited duration of their flight. Whether these objects would be considered as space crafts or aircrafts is unclear. It may be noted that these deficiencies may, to a certain extent, be cured by the adoption of the 'Mission Intent Line' as proposed by Thomas Gangale. He argues that it is the planned destination of the airborne object that should define its classification as a spacecraft or aircraft.[115] Establishing the destination of the object may help establish the nature of the activity to be carried out. However, this would require recognition of spacialist principles.

Furthermore, what amounts to 'space activity' remains undefined. Defining the extent of 'space activity' may prove to be a more tedious task then delimiting a physical boundary. It may also lead to prolonged and complex legal issues especially when ascertaining liability of a party is concerned.

Another practical consideration that must be addressed is the blurring of boundaries between usual air transportation and suborbital flights. The view of the ICAO is that the functionalist school will apply air law to both since the focal area of operation is air space and any excursion into outer space is merely incidental to its flight through air space. Hence, in the view of the functionalist school it must be the air

---

[115] *Supra* note 64, at 17

space regime that would be applicable to both. The issue with this interpretation is that it puts both conventional air flights and sub orbital flights on the same pedestal. This is in many ways unfair. It treats unlike alike. The regime does not fulfil the basic norm of natural justice. By fixing a common pedestal for unlike acts it perpetuates an unequal application of law.

Spatialist theory

The spatialist theory seeks to delimit the boundary of outer space at a fixed and definitive altitude. The spatialist approach relies on environmental criteria and therefore would eliminate ambiguities in ascertaining the applicable jurisdiction. However, ascertaining the environmental criteria has been a hotly debated question especially since it may trespass upon State sovereignty. These proposals have been varied, ranging from the Lagrange points of the Earth proposed by Joseph Kroell to the "Biological Jurisdictional Line" proposed by Marcel le Goff.[116]

Like with the functionalist theory, it may also be argued that the spatialist theory does enjoy an implied acceptance in international law. The recognition or maintenance of special interests of certain States over areas beyond their territory is one that enjoys substantial precedent. [117] Land boundaries and maritime boundaries including the EEZ and continental shelf are spatially delimited.

An often-cited method of delimitation is the Von Karman line at a height of 100Km. This line is generally considered the point at which the

---

[116] Gangale, *Supra* note 60, at 95, 97
[117] Oduntan, *Supra* note 48, at 301

atmosphere ceases to possess sufficient gas and density to sustain the flight of balloons and aircrafts.[118] It may be pointed out that balloons are considered as aircrafts by the ICAO.[119] States are bound to view the delimitation of airspace from the prism of national security. It has been pointed out that there does exist a height above 100km where aircrafts can fly and atmospheric resistance is not sufficient to disintegrate satellites (or weapons) due to friction.[120] In such a scenario an arguably outdated limit such as the Von Karman line would be redundant.

Despite the numerous methods of delimitation propounded, the political nature of delimitation cannot be ignored. Oduntan writes "the reason why the indecision over the issue of spatial demarcation has been allowed to fester so long is because the absence of a precise boundary is advantageous to the dominant interests in international space exploration."[121] Despite this there has been a tacit understanding as to the height of delimitation. In 1960 when a U-2 spy plane (having a maximum altitude of 70,000 Feet) of the United States was shot down over the USSR, the USA did not contest the territorial sovereignty of the USSR at that height. In the case of Nicaragua v. USA the ICJ held that similar

---

[118] Oduntan, *Supra* note 48, at 157
[119] *Supra* note 114.
[120] Oduntan, *Supra* note 48
[121] Oduntan, *Supra* note 48, at 61

reconnaissance flights over Nicaraguan airspace were a violation of Nicaragua's territorial sovereignty.[122] In 2009 a DPRK satellite launch vehicle passed 400Km over Japan. Again that year another of DPRK's satellite launch vehicle passed 280Km over Japan. In both these instances, though Japan sent a diplomatic protest to DPRK, it did not claim a violation of its airspace. According to the Japanese defence ministry's white paper "No clear international agreement has been reached on the definition of outer space, though it is generally considered as located 100 km or further away from the Earth's surface."[123] Therefore, there is an understanding, though imprecise, of the spatial delimitation of outer space.

The Bogota Declaration[124] of 1976 also highlights the political nature of determining special boundaries. Eight equatorial States sought to extend their sovereignty up to the geostationary orbit at a distance of 36,000Km. The claim of sovereignty was not received well by either developed or developing countries. It may also be argued that the Bogota declaration is a contravention of the OST as it would hinder the "free exploration of outer space."

---

[122] *Nicaragua v. United States of America* 986 I.C.J. 14
[123] Ministry of Defense (Japan), *Defense of Japan 2014*, Part 1, Chapter 2, Section 4, available at: https://warp.da.ndl.go.jp/info:ndljp/pid/11591426/www.mod.go.jp/e/publ/w_paper/pdf/2014/DOJ2014_1-2-4_web_1031.pdf (last visited May 4, 2022).
[124] The 1976 Declaration of the First Meeting of Equatorial Countries, Dec 3, 1976

In conclusion, while a relatively precise boundary may be decided upon, the application of a legal regime while the space craft is passing through airspace must still be addressed. It is likely that this would require closer cooperation between the ICAO and the UNCOPUS. "Integration of higher airspace operations with global air navigation systems" is a potential issue that must be deliberated upon. [125] Furthermore, the sovereign right of a state to defend itself must be factored into while deciding upon an agreeable height for delimitation. It is unlikely that these issues would be resolved anytime in the near future in light of its implications.

---

[125] International Civil Aviation Organization Secretariat, *Operations Above Flight Level 600*, 2 (ICAO Working Paper AN-Conf/13-WP/16 12/6/18), available at: https://www.icao.int/Meetings/anconf13/Documents/WP/wp_016_en.pdf (last visited May 4, 2022).

Issues plaguing the spatialist school

Spatialists also suffer from a lack of agreement amongst themselves. In 1966 these divisions were apparent and so was the lack of an agreement among the member States favouring the spatialist view. The spatialist school due to its very nature attracts a plethora of methodologies for delimitation. It also concerns itself with the delimitation of national air space from international airspace, and even from outer space. Hence, there are those who propose bi-zonal, tri-zonal, and even plurizonal solutions.[126] Bin Cheng comments that there are "there are probably as many criteria as there are speakers or writers on the subject."[127] This comment is tragicomic in the sense that the while spatialist share a general consensus on the matter they have failed to agree upon one specific methodology. The irony perhaps is that their 'plurizonal solutions' have become 'plurizonal dilemmas'. In fairness there is naturally a need to identify a methodology that will stand the test of time.

There are also more practical considerations that the international community would have to seriously

---

[126] Cheng, *Supra* note 96, at 2
[127] *Id.*

ponder over. One matter that may seem like an overly scrupulous and tiresome exercise, is the scenario in which an object is near the point of delimitation (on either side) and a dispute arises in which establishing the exact location at which such dispute arose would be incredibly difficult. At speeds of nearly 28,400 kilometres per hour (orbital velocity) or more while crossing a theoretically width-less line would be incredibly challenging.

The pragmatic complexities of the situation boggle the mind. In fact in its submission Greece had noted that low speed of objects on *terra firma* and the open seas allows for the application of dualism.[128] In a situation where a buffer zone a few kilometres wide exists, the situation only gets more complicated. In such an instance not only would the distance be covered in a matter of a few milliseconds but the buffer zone would may also require the establishment of a *sui generis* legal regime. Nevertheless, to be fair it must be mentioned that applying different legal fictions to the same object and thereby subjecting it to a different legal regime has precedent.

In the early days of seaplanes this question arose in the case of *Reinhardt v. Newport Flying Service Corp.*[129] In

---

[128] UNCOPUOS, Questionnaire on Possible Legal Issues with Regard to Aerospace Objects: Replies from member States, U.N Doc. A/AC.105/635/Add.3, 4, available at A/AC.105/635/Add.3 (unoosa.org) (last visited Apr 30, 2022).

[129] *Reinhardt v. Newport Flying Service Corp.*, 133 N.E. 371 (NY, 1921).

this particular the case the position of an amphibious vehicle had come into question. Judge Cardozo in this particular matter held that the hydroplane while it was moored, anchored or navigated itself on navigable waters was subject to the jurisdiction of the admiralty court as a maritime vessel instead of an aircraft. However the judge further pointed out that while the hydroplane was in the air it would not be subject to the jurisdiction of the admiralty court nor be considered as a maritime vessel. Similarly it is not beyond the realm of imagination for an aircraft to be treated as a space craft after it crosses the point of delimitation.

Another matter that should be considered is the position of a space object that intends to enter suborbital space for a miniscule amount of time.[130] SpaceShipOne is a quintessential example. Other object that will give further impetus to arriving at a solution are sounding rockets, and military suborbital flights which include among other things, Inter-Continental Ballistic Missiles (ICBM), and Anti-Satellite (ASAT) Weapons. In such scenarios where an object remains in outer space only for a few seconds to a few minutes the functionalist school of thought would cover such an object under the legal regime governing air space. It has been noted even by the ICAO that the spatialist school lacks clarity on this matter thereby hindering the identification of a legal regime that must be applied. It, however, notes

---

[130] *Supra* note 14, at 222

that the functionalist school air law would be the applicable regime since "airspace would be the main centre of activities of sub-orbital vehicles in the course of an earth-to-earth transportation, any crossing of outer space being brief and only incidental to the flight."[131]

On the other hand the spacialist school would require that two different legal regimes established by two different organizations -The ICAO in case of air law and the UN or some other future body in case of space law- be applied on the object.[132] The difficulty posed by the adoption of the spatialist school is made discernible by the above-mentioned illustrations.

---

[131] Commercial Space Flights, LC/36-WP/3-2, *in* Legal Committee – 36th Session, 5, (2015), available at: https://www.icao.int/Meetings/LC36/Working%20Papers/LC%2036%20-%20WP%203-2.en.pdf (last visited May 1, 2022).

[132] *Supra* note 14, at 222.

Resolving The Functionalist And Spacialist Conflict

Harmonious Construction.

The question that begets us now is as to which theory would suit the future of space exploration and benefit the exploration of the common heritage of mankind. Adoption of any one theory would perhaps fundamentally change the legal regime we exist in. However, it also becomes apparent that the current legal regime established by the outer space treaty and all the consecutive treaties that followed it have not adopted a single theory. This may appear to resolve issues arising out of space exploration but establishing the point of delimitation becomes even more complex as it must base itself on a spatialist or functionalist mode of determination.

The lack of definitions and the almost purposeful ambiguity of the terms and definitions makes it even tougher to understand the intentions of the high contracting parties. For instance, the functionalist perspective would require a clear definition of 'space object' however the Convention on International Liability for Damage Caused by Space Objects defines it as "The term "space object" includes component parts of a space object as well as its launch vehicle and parts thereof". The parties to the treaty either purposefully chose to ignore the definition or assumed that the definition was implicit to the extent that only the ambiguity surrounding a part of a space object should have been cleared. This ambiguity is a microcosm of a much larger issue at hand, that is of the lack of any "point of departure or reference for a definition" [133] This issue was realized when the subcommittee was informed that "there were no scientific or technical criteria even provisional in nature, which could be taken as a point of departure or reference for a definition."[134]

Importantly, there is also a lack of definition of 'aerospace' object. It is the aerospace object that forms the marrow of this bone of contention between the functionalist and spatialist schools. From a lay man's point of view an aerospace object is a hybrid object that can travel through both air space and outer space. Hence, it is an object that can like an aircraft use aerodynamic lift while in airspace and other means of propulsion while in outer space. Therefore all aerospace vehicles or objects are also space objects and aircrafts depending upon the region

---

[133] UNCOPUOS, The Question of The Definition And/Of the Delimitation of Outer Space, U.N Doc. A_AC-105_C-2_7_Add-1, 8, available at
https://digitallibrary.un.org/record/741816?ln=en (last visited Apr 30, 2022).
[134] *Id.*

they operate.[135] Though this may not be necessarily true since a functionalist interpretation of the true nature of the objection would depend on the mission of the aerospace object.

Furthermore, the Rescue Agreement and Registration Convention by their very nature are applicable to space objects regardless of where they are, as opposed to outer space as such. It must be emphasised that these regimes, are "important functionalist exceptions to the spatialist 'rule'". This is partly one of the underlying causes for the conflict between the spatialism and functionalist school. This may very well be identified as one of the reasons for the inability of the international community in arriving at a point of delimitation or even a methodology for arriving at the application of a legal regime on an object.[136]

The method to solve this would necessitate reworking how we perceive it. It is not unfathomable that functionalist treaties can exist alongside a legal regime that delimits outer space based on a spatialist approach. For instance "by their very nature the legal regimes of Rescue Agreement and Registration Convention attach to space objects largely irrespective of where they are, as opposed to outer space as such. Not only are these regimes important functionalist exceptions to the spatialist 'rule', but they are also the underlying cause for the whole spatialism and

---

[135] *Supra* note 14, at 213
[136] Gangale, *Supra* note 60, at 414

functionalism debate. It is also responsible for the fact that no borderline between outer space and airspace has yet been drawn."[137] Here it is also relevant to point out that the idea for a technological criterion was shot down since "no science was or could be dependent on technology."[138]

Proponents of both theories have sought to reject the idea of the other citing examples in various situations and also the treaties that form the foundation of international space law. The example of SpaceShip1 has been cited as a 'rejection' of the functionalist approach.[139] The reason being that it achieves suborbital flight; that is to say that it 'flies' higher than an aircraft but does not enter into an orbit around the earth. Taking the example of SpaceShipOne the conundrum becomes evident. While Space Ship 1 has been registered as a reusable rocket by the United States Federal Aviation Administration the 'rocket' has not been registered as a space object.

It appears that the said rocket is not a non-space object that does enter space albeit briefly. It is also relevant to point out that Article II the Registration convention describes only those objects which are

---

[137] *Supra* note 81, at 256

[138] UNCOPUOS, The Question of The Definition And/Of the Delimitation of Outer Space, U.N Doc. A_AC-105_C-2_7_Add-1, 8, available at

https://digitallibrary.un.org/record/741816?ln=en (last visited Apr 30, 2022).

[139] Rhys Monahan, *The sky's the limit? Establishing a legal delimitation of airspace and outer space* 32, 2008, available at:

http://etheses.dur.ac.uk/2248/ ((last visited May 4, 2022).

launched into 'Earth orbit or beyond' as space objects. Nevertheless, the term 'or beyond' does further complicate matters. For instance, in a hypothetical situation that an object like SpaceShipOne travelled a considerable distance and returned back to Earth without entering into orbit then would such an object still not be a space object. However, to play the devil's advocate reliance can be placed on the definition of 'Deep Space' adopted at the 1963 conference of the International Radio Consultative Committee (CCIR) of the International Telecommunications Union which defined Deep Space as "Space at distances from earth equal to or greater than the distance between the earth and the moon."[140]

The absurdity becomes more apparent when one realises that the whole *raison detre* of SpaceShipOne was to provide an experience of outer space. Space ship one is also not merely entering outer space. It is also travelling through air space as it approaches its destination. Would it not then be fair to treat is as aircraft or must one create a separate legal fiction to treat an air craft as a space craft merely because it was intended to be used as a space craft. It is also relevant to point out that since according to the ICAO for an object to be deemed to be an aircraft it must make use of aerodynamic flight, SpaceShipOne does not qualify as an aircraft since it uses 'force against the

---

[140] *Supra* note 138.

Earth'.[141] Furthermore, "being a 'rocket' does not necessarily denote SpaceShipOne as a spacecraft, as there is no formal definition".[142]

Despite these differences there still does not appear any reason why there cannot be a harmonious construction and consequent adoption of these theories simultaneously by the international community. Various aspects of the functionalist school and the spatialist school can be adopted and constructively be amalgamated so as to form a harmonious unison which can birth a legal regime *sui generis* to outer space. It can be another legal innovation of the human species that would further aid the human species in exploring and perhaps in colonizing the Solar System.

Bin Cheng shares a similar view. According to him the functionalist apprehension of the spatialist view is unjustified as spatialism "does not mean doing away with a functional classification of what is a lawful activity and what is not, but to apply a functional test without regard to where an activity takes place is not only to put the cart before the horse, but to dispense with the horse."[143]

Writing on assigning legality or illegality, Bin Cheng is of the view that the said legality of an act may have less to do with the act itself and may have more to do with the location or area from where the act is done. This may not necessarily hold true. Cybercrime is

---

[141] *Supra* note 139, at 34
[142] *Id.*
[143] Cheng, *Supra* note 96, at 8

illegal despite the fact that it may not have been physically or even virtually affect a nation or its citizens. Nevertheless, in the context of delimitation of outer space the argument has some merit.

Resolving the conflict

The matter of State sovereignty may perhaps only partly answer the question of where the legal regime governing airspace ends and that which governs outer space begins. It is not necessary that State sovereignty must accompany the jurisdictional limits of airspace. They overlap and form subsets but are neither wholly mutually inclusive nor mutually exclusive. It will do us good to remove the notion that State sovereignty is an appendage of airspace. Such a notion may be true only with respect to the lateral boundaries of air space. This faulty notion can inhibit the flexibility that legal fictions can provide in adequately addressing the issue of delimitation of air space and outer space. The question that the international community has failed to unanimously solve is of course that of delimitation but it is relevant for us to analyse the friction, if any, that persists between the legal regimes governing airspace and outer space. Today both areas are governed by their own set of international conventions which though may be harmoniously existing, fail to provide a gradual transition or buffer between both regimes. An analysis of the conventions dealing with both regimes makes the matter apparent. The treaties governing air space are as follows:

1. Paris Convention of 1919 (addressing safety and navigation),
2. Warsaw Convention of 1929 (addressing air carrier liability to passengers and cargo),
3. Rome Convention of 1933 (addressing liability for surface damage caused by aircraft)
4. Chicago Convention of 1944 (addressing safety and navigation),
5. Geneva Convention of 1948 (addressing aircraft registration),
6. Hague Protocol (addressing air carrier liability to passengers and cargo),
7. Rome Convention of 1952 (addressing aircraft operator liability for surface damage),
8. Guadalajara Convention (addressing air carrier liability to passengers and cargo),
9. Tokyo Convention of 1963 (addressing offenses on board aircraft),
10. Montreal Protocols of 1966 (addressing air carrier liability to passengers and cargo)
11. Hague Convention of 1970 (addressing aircraft hijacking),
12. Montreal Convention of 1971 (addressing aircraft and air navigation security)
13. The Montreal Protocol of 1988 (addressing airport security)
14. Montreal Convention of 1999 (addressing air carrier liability to passengers and cargo)
15. Cape Town Convention of 2001 (addressing financial interests in aircraft)

16. Montreal Conventions of 2009 (addressing liability for surface damage)
17. Beijing Convention and Protocol of 2010 (addressing security)

Meanwhile the treaties governing Outer space are as follows:

1. Treaty on Principles Governing the Activities of States in the Exploration and Use of Outer Space, Including the Moon and Other Celestial Bodies, 27 January 1967, 610 UNTS 205
2. Agreement on the Rescue of Astronauts, the Return of Astronauts and the Return of Objects Launched into Outer Space, 22 April 1968, 672 UNTS
3. Convention on International Liability for Damage Caused by Space Objects, 29 March 1972, 961 UNTS 187
4. Convention on Registration of Objects Launched into Outer Space, 6 June 1975, 28 UST 695, 1023 UNTS 15
5. Agreement Governing the Activities of States on the Moon and Other Celestial Bodies, 5 December 1979, 1363 UNTS 3

An analysis of the above mentioned, rather a mere perusal of the names of the above-mentioned treaties makes the vast gap in regulation of outer space apparent. It also makes the lack of smooth transition between both legal regimes apparent on the face of it. This also serves as one of the points of friction not merely between the legal regimes applicable to air space and outer space but also the friction that exists between the functionalists and spatialists schools of thought. The daunting challenge of working around a seemingly black and white legal regime having sharp distinctions is clearly a factor in the stagnant evolution of delimitation of outer space.

The notion of sovereignty over air space developed as a customary law after the First World War. It was recognized as an 'obvious' extension of State sovereignty. The evolution of technology, particularly military aviation technology ensured that not much resistance was faced by this idea. It's place as an international customary law was ensured. Looking back from the 21st century, it of course seems like *fait accompli*. While initially it may seem that establishing the legal and jurisdictional origins of airspace law may provide us a head start of preparing a foundation for outer space law, this idea may very well be a flawed notion. Outer space law so far has no precedent upon which it can establish its existence. One probable solution that could be offered to this is to delimit outer space by exclusion. That is to say, what is not airspace is outer space. The most apparent and obvious issue with this is that it oversimplifies the matter. Is it, however, wrong to delimit or even assume that space beyond air space is outer space? An issue may arise where a 'trizonal' or 'plurizonal' solution is offered. However, in the eventuality that a delimitation by exclusion is considered, it may not be wholly incorrect to say that the origins of outer space law may lie in customary law by implication.

While establishing the upper limits of national airspace, in light of the fact that the Chicago convention had failed to do so, reliance could be placed on the most obvious and natural meaning of the word 'Air Space'. The Permanent Court of International Justice considered a similar question in the Eastern Greenland Case (1933).[144] In this case the court while interpreting the word 'Greenland' and by extension the boundaries of Greenland. After placing reliance of official documentation and various diplomatic documents the court came to the conclusion that the 'natural meaning' of Greenland would also be the 'geographical meaning'.[145] Bin Cheng is of the view that this interpretation would be applicable to the term 'airspace'. Hence, in his view airspace would denote the region of space where atmosphere exists. To prevent any reduction of logic to the limits of absurdity it may be said that more precisely airspace refers to that region of atmospheric space which can sustain flight.

Having delineated airspace it can be said that that region of space which does not have substantial

---

[144] Cheng, *Supra* note 59, at 2
[145] Legal Status Of Eastern Greenland. (Norway V. Denmark). Permanent Court of International Justice, 1933. [1933] P.C.I.J, p. 52

atmosphere for flight constitutes outer space or in the case of a plurizonal delimitation, a region to which airspace law does not extend. However, State sovereignty need not be limited to airspace. The outer space treaty makes it clear that national sovereignty does not extend to outer space. In the eventuality that a plurizonal delimitation occurs and outer space is not established by exclusion of airspace, national sovereignty may very well extend into what can be perhaps be described as near space.

Having stressed upon the natural meaning of the term it is important to highlight that a mutually agreeable interpretation of a concept or a boundary is not unheard of. It is rather common for delineation of boundaries to occur by mutual agreement. Bin Cheng cites the views of Judge Humber in the *Palmas Case* of 1928 in which Huber J. stated that territorial sovereignty "serves to divide between nations the space upon which human activities are employed," he further went on to state that where a boundary by its very own is unable to secure such a division it is bound to attract controversy. Arriving at a general agreement is therefore important in the view of Cheng.[146]

An international law traces its origin to, among other things, customary law and agreements between States. Observance of these rules, reciprocity, and consistent application of these norms lead to the creation of a

---

[146] Cheng, *Supra* note 59, at 3

norm of international law. Hence, where a legal fiction is introduced, which may be contrary to the normal and geographical meaning of a term, the legal fiction will persist since it was the intention of the parties to do so, in the light of lack of ambiguity surrounding the term. The Convention on the Continental Shelf of 1958 [147] Article 1 of which defines the term 'continental shelf' in accordance with the mutually agreed interpretation of the term rather than relying on the normal or geographical meaning of the term 'continental shelf'. Similarly, Article 2(3) of the convention seek to make clear the extension of the right of a sovereign State over the continental shelf despite what would normally be considered a defect in the exercise of sovereignty owing to a lack of "occupation, effective or notional, or on any express proclamation."[148] The convention goes on to further delineate the extent of the State's sovereignty, Article 3 of the convention limits the extent of the State's sovereignty over the "superjacent waters as high seas, or that of the airspace above those waters." This may have occurred due to the existing rights of the costal state over the continental shelf.

It is clear that States can agree on limiting their own sovereignty by agreement and even unilaterally since it is an exercise of sovereignty. Bin Cheng raises a pertinent question on this subject which holds an important place in the larger discussion surrounding

---

[147] *Supra* note 2, Art. 2
[148] *Id.*

the delimitation of outer space. He asks whether "whether States may, even by agreement, extend their national sovereignty beyond the terrestrial atmosphere."[149] It is a fact that States agreed upon the notion of 'common heritage of mankind' by mutual agreement. It is hence a legal fiction that states cannot claim areas of outer space or celestial bodies. However, if hypothetically States agreed upon altering this legal fiction or in the least allow for an extension of national sovereignty in near space would such an agreement be valid? To quote Cheng again "International law is not made by the will of international lawyers. It is made by the will of States. If States wish to create a right of transit passage for space flights through the airspace of other States, or if they wish to abolish airspace sovereignty of States altogether in favour of foreign space flights, they are perfectly entitled to attempt to do so." [150] Furthermore it must be noted that while a distinction may be made by legislation or otherwise, a State may still choose to exercise jurisdiction regardless. This is true for two reasons. Firstly, as mentioned above States have the right to decide their own jurisdiction and secondly the *corpus juris spatialis internationalis* or fundamental laws governing space which consists of

---

[149] Cheng, *Supra* note 59, at 4

[150] Bin Cheng, *The Legal Status of Outer Space and Relevant Issues: Delimitation of Outer Space and Definition of Peaceful Use*, 11 Journal of Space Law 97 (1983),
https://heinonline.org/HOL/LandingPage?handle=hein.journals/jrlsl11&div=16&id=&page= (last visited May 5, 2022).

the five treaties pertaining to outer space, they have also as an international community, adopted both spatialist and functionalist approaches towards establishing jurisdiction over outer space and outer space activities.

Cheng consequently makes a comparison between outer space and the high seas, both of which are *res communis*. The Geneva conference of 1958 and 1960 extend the limit of the territorial sea at the expense of the high seas which is and was, the common heritage of mankind. The Territorial Sea was at the time of conception extending only up to 3 Nautical Miles from the shore line. Today it extends to 12 nautical miles. Here, on a related note, the views of Ram Jhaku may be noted. He takes the example of the arbitrary extension of the territorial sea by various states which was resolved by the Law of the Sea Convention. [151] Similarly, can the international community not by agreement extend the sovereignty of nations into outer space. Such an extension of sovereignty need not be unqualified and may come along with limitation just as the rights associated with the continental shelf.

---

[151] Ram Jakhu, *Legal Issues Relating to the Global Public Interest in Outer Space*, 2005, 55-56. Available at: Current Legal Issues Relating to Access to Space* (umd.edu) (last visited Apr 30, 2022).

Role of the ICAO

With regards to the question of deciding the governing authority for aerospace objects, considering the unique nature of an aerospace object, another matter arises before us. That is, whether the ICAO has the jurisdiction to regulate aerospace objects? This question would answer the approach the international community would take while regulating aerospace objects. There is a difference between the term 'aircraft' as defined in Article 3(a) of the Chicago Convention and as defined in the Annexes of the convention. [152] It has been contend that the term 'aircraft' used in the former provision includes within its ambit Sub-Orbital aerospace transportation vehicles (SATVs). The authors of the paper were of the view that there are two questions involved here. One, whether Sub-Orbital aerospace transportation vehicles are covered under Article 3(a) of the convention, if this question is answered in the negative the second question arises whether Sub-Orbital aerospace transportation vehicles should be covered under Article 3(a) of the convention. The first question is a question of law while the second

---

[152] Space Safety Regulations and Standards, 246 (Joseph Pelton & Ram Jakhu 1 ed. 2010).

question is one of policy. To answer the former question the authors relied on the raison d'être of the Chicago convention. They highlighted that one of the purposes mentioned in the preamble of the convention was to ensure "safe and orderly" [153] manner of international civil aviation, and ensure that "International air transport services may be established on the basis of equality of opportunity and operated soundly and economically."[154]

Since the purpose of the convention is to create a "harmonious regime of safety and navigation of airspace" the convention would by implication seek to regulate aerospace objects at least for the duration of their flight through airspace. Safety and navigation of airspace cannot be siloed. Emphasis must be placed on a wholistic view of airspace safety which would by implication require a wider interpretation of the term aircraft as mentioned in Article 3(a).

Where a legal interpretation of the term aircraft fails to cover aerospace, the international community must consider it a matter of policy to amend the provision so as to cover aerospace objects within its ambit. The alternative could perhaps be to introduce the term aerospace in the Chicago convention keeping in mind the proliferation of aerospace objects and the need to secure air space. It cannot be said that the drafters of the convention did not intend to cover aerospace objects within the ambit of the convention. What can

---

[153] Preamble to Chicago convention
[154] Preamble to Chicago convention

be said with certainty is that at the time of the drafting of the convention aerospace object were few and far in-between. An example maybe cited to make the absurdity of not covering SATVs within the ambit of the term aircraft. In this example both an aircraft and a SATV are travelling at an altitude of 20,000 feet to transport passengers.[155] The lacuna facing the ICAO in this scenario is that while both crafts are performing the same function, the SATV is not subject to the regulations laid down by the ICAO merely due to the designation of 'aerospace' object attached to it. The Chicago convention by virtue of the intention of the contracting States have granted the ICAO the authority to regulate Sub-Orbital aerospace transportation vehicles. They state that this view holds true even when the ambiguity and *prima facie* conflict of laws is apparent with regards to the legal regime applicable to a region or on the vehicle in question.[156]

The ICAO has also recognised its own role in matters of international civil aviation related to matters of outer space. It has in pursuance of fulfilling this role urged member States to keep the organization informed of the States "programmes and the progress achieved in the exploration and use of outer space."[157]

---

[155] *Supra* note 152, at 247
[156] *Supra* note 152, at 251
[157] International Civil Aviation Organization, Resolutions Adopted by The Assembly and Index to Documentation 71, 72

Dr. Nandasiri Jasentuliyana has also stressed on the need for the ICAO to provide a 'clarification' if the COPUOS continues to fail to reach a mutual consensus amongst member states as it has for the past thirty years.

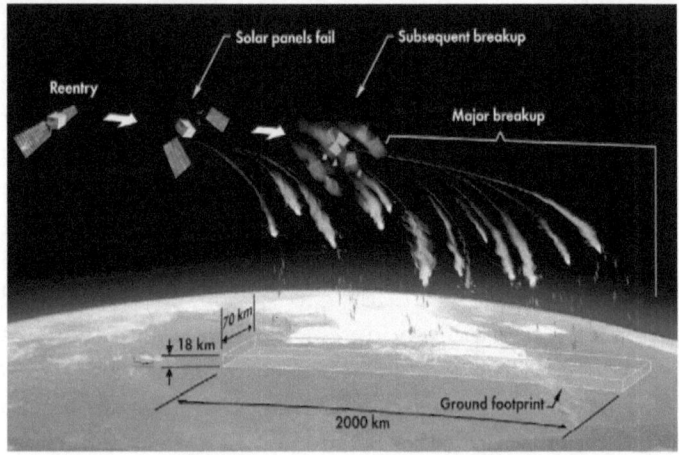

Figure 4 : Risk posed to Outer space and airspace due to debris.[158]

(1992), available at: https://www.icao.int/assembly-archive/Session29/A.29.RESOL.9600.EN.pdf (last visited May 1, 2022).
[158] *Supra* note 152, at 262

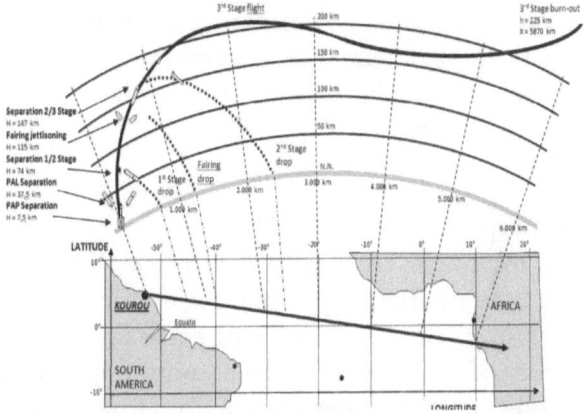

Figure 5: Expected range of debris during launch.[159]

The above two images show that debris during launch or during an inadvertent, controlled or uncontrolled destruction of a space object would pose a threat to outer space, the buffer zone, and air space below. The issue is not merely limit to the vertical plane. It is in fact more pronounced in the horizontal plane. From the illustrations above we can note that portions of a space shuttle upon separation at an altitude of 150 kilometres can cause debris to travel nearly 1,500 kilometres in the horizontal plane. When launches are conducted by smaller nations, and those not having access to large open seas in the flight path of their

---

[159] Marietta Benkö & Engelhard Plescher, Space law 12 (2013).

launches. The cooperation of the international community gains significance as the number of launches increases. Transparency, reduction of information asymmetry, and general safety are matters that would naturally arise as protocols are agreed upon in the future.

This is particularly important because regulation is not meant to merely cover jurisdictional issues and liability issues pertaining to the object. General safety of outer space or near space is of equal importance to the safety of airspace. It is hence important either to have one unified organization or for a synergy between the ICAO and COPUOS.

The following concerns, *inter alia*, may be identified as involving the safety of outer space, inner space and airspace:

a) High Altitude platform stations (HAPS)[160]
b) "High-altitude pseudo-satellites are under manufacture and testing, demonstrating the ability to travel long distances for extended periods of time at altitudes higher than those reached by traditional aircraft

---

[160] UNCOPUOS, Information relating to any practical case known that would warrant the definition and delimitation of outer space, U.N Doc. A/AC.105/1226/Add.1, 3, available at https://www.unoosa.org/oosa/oosadoc/data/documents/2021/aac.105/aac.1051226add.1_0.html, (last visited Apr 30, 2022).

c) Sizeable anthropogenic debris below the Karman line, registered with the United Nations

d) Suborbital flight tests are increasingly proving the technological readiness of private companies to offer suborbital transportation;

e) The very low Earth orbit is garnering interest for Earth observation and telecommunication purposes, narrowing the gap between activities in upper airspace and the lowest perigee that is technologically possible."[161]

The very nature of the above listed matters is such that they warrant the active role of the ICAO even though they may not directly be within the spatial jurisdiction of the ICAO for an extended period of time. It also goes without saying that where the said object finds itself in the buffer zone yet vertically above territorial airspace then it also becomes the duty of the launching state and of the international community to reassure the state upon which such object passes over. For the benefit of transparency, peace, and harmony among nations and for lasting peace in the common heritage of mankind, that is outer space, sharing of information concerning the location and nature of such object gains primacy.

---

[161] *Id.*

Discovering Neutralia

Shared Commonalities with maritime Law and establishment of Neutralia.

An analysis of the subject thoroughly leads us to a never ending and almost tragicomic set of rebuttals and surrebuttals. Despite this the solution to the question may already exist before us. Firstly, it is important to consider what challenges need to be addressed before a viable solution is suggested. The following challenges may be listed as follows:

a) The method of delimitation must adhere to a minimum standard of scientific and technical checks.

b) It must be able to cover all kinds of vehicles including air crafts and aerospace vehicles and space craft.

c) The methodology should factor in the safety and security of the airspace.

d) It must not prejudice national security subject to rational limitations.

e) It should preferably have precedent in international law.

f) It must withstand the test of reasonableness.

g) It must be a solution that can either adapt to technological changes without altering its form or be sound enough to exist regardless of technological evolution.

h) Avoiding abrupt delimitations so as to avoid complex spatial issues.

On consideration of these factors one precedent of delimitation that satisfies these conditions largely, is the maritime delimitation of the seas. Presently the United Nations Convention on the Law of the Seas delimits the maritime regions into numerous parts based on their relation to unsubmerged land. The UNCLOS seeks to delimit the areas of the seas, and assigns States and the international community rights and duties based on this delimitation. These delimitations also ensure that the national and costal security of the State along with the law and order of the region is ensured without prejudice to the rights of the State. Maritime delimitation has evolved considerably but its very nature itself has remained constant. It has withstood the test of time and today is nearly universally accepted. Even a relatively new concept of the continental shelf has gained universal acceptance within a relatively short span of time.[162] While it is true that states have often had an umpteen number of disputes concerning maritime boundaries and have at times resorted to violence, the fact of the

---

[162] H.O Agarwal, International law and Human Rights 139 (20 ed. 2015).

matter is that an adequet resort to justice and fair adjudication of the matter exists and functions.

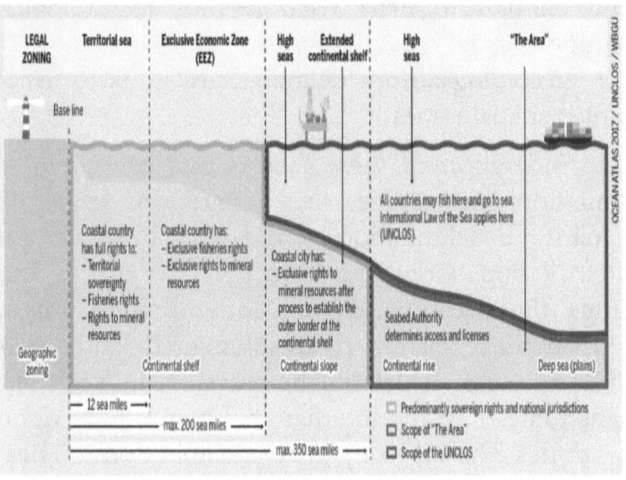

Figure 6: Delimitation of the Seas [163]

The international tribunal for the law of the seas (ITLOS), the permenant court of arbitration and the international court of Justice particularly have dealt with matters pertaining to the maritime domain. While there are still concerns that haunt the maritime

---

[163] Bas Bolman et al., Oceans Report - Addressing SDG14 issues with factual data and state of the art knowledge. 8 (2022), available at:
https://www.researchgate.net/publication/331928317_Oceans_Report_-_Addressing_SDG14_issues_with_factual_data_and_state_of_the_art_knowledge (last visited May 1, 2022).

domain and stake holders, the fact of the matter remains that the maritime domain is relatively well regulated with the rule of law being upheld across the globe by the international community. Countering piracy across the globe especially in the Persian gulf and the Arabian sea is characteristic of the will of the international community in tackling the problems that plaugue the 'commons'. The ability to tackle the problems of the common and by implication countering the tragedy of the commons is a product of convention, and customs that have the near unanimous acceptace of the international community in letter and spirit.

It is crucial to recognize the cause for the widespread acceptance for the UNCLOS. According to Oduntant the reason for the acceptance and mainitaince of such 'special zones' is due to the "underlying legal logic" of justice and equitability.[164] Hence, the law of the seas can serve as a viable blueprint that can be adopted for the delimitation of the outer space. Notable examples include the Exclusive Economic Zone (EEZ), the Continental Shelf. Environmental concerns have even spurned the creation of large marine ecosystem (LME) and Particularly Sensitive Sea Area (PSSA).[165]

The importance of an intermediate zone that will prevent complexities of a spatial nature cannot be emphasised enough. The maritime regime despite the slow speed of vessels is a case in point of the need for

---

[164] Oduntan, *Supra* note 48, at 302
[165] *Id.*

a buffer zone to prevent an abrupt application of legal regimes. An intermediate zone between airspace and outer space prevents an abrupt delimitation between these two zones. In the Law of the Seas the EEZ prevents an abrupt delimitation between territorial waters and the high sea. An intermediate zone has proved to ensure peaceful settlement of disputes. Such a concept has been deliberated upon in the past.

Thomas Gangale suggests the same as a probable form of delimitation. This plurizonal method of delmtation can be found in the Magna Carta of Space which was adopted by the Inter-American Bar Association in February 1961. In particular, Article 8 of the declaration proposed the establishment of a neutral zone embracing the upper limits of Air Space and the lower limits of Outer Space referred to as 'Neutralia'. In this zone it was proposed that there would be the right to innocent passage for all crafts and objects and that such passage would not be deemed to be a violation of State sovereignty.[166]

---

[166] Gangale, *Supra* note 60, at 87

UPPER AND LOWER LIMITS OF NEUTRALIA PROPOSED BY SCHOLARS

Name of Scholar	Lower Limit (Km)	Upper Limit (Km)
Oduntan[167]	88.5	160.9
Hyman[168][169]	84.5 120.7 965.6	241.4 956.6 8,046
C. de Jager and G. Reijnen[170]	50	130

The establishment of a buffer zone serves numerous purposes. Firstly, it assures states of their complete territorial sovereignty up to a height. Secondly, it "accommodates further scientific discoveries, which may necessitate an increase in the area recognised as airspace or a lowering of the precise limits of outer

---

[167] Gangale, *Supra* Note 60, at 88
[168] Hyman Proposed three options.
[169] Gangale, *Supra* Note 60, at 88
[170] UNCOPUOS, The Question of The Definition And/Of the Delimitation of Outer Space, U.N Doc. A_AC-105_C-2_7_Add-1, 24, available at https://digitallibrary.un.org/record/741816?ln=en (last visited Apr 30, 2022).

space."[171] Oduntan even suggests that a buffer zone may serve as a political bargaining chip for States in their international relations.[172] It may be worth noting that here that many of these benefits of establishing a 'Neutralia' are similar to those provided in Chapter V of the UNCLOS.[173] This buffer zone would be a region above territorial airspace and below outer space, and would be considered to be international airspace.[174] Unlike the Exclusive Economic Zone which is effectively a buffer zone, it is still not recognised as international waters. Neutralia on the other hand would be a buffer zone and international airspace concomitantly. One rationale for this discrepancy is the fact that unlike the sea which is rich with resources and is teeming with marine life, the upper edges of air space is, with the exception of some bacteria and non-economical particulates, baren and inhospitable. It is unlikely to anticipate any commercial resource that can be harvested or extracted. Of course, until such a scenario becomes probable.

The concept of 'Neutralia' is similar to 'Mesospace' that had been suggested by professor C. de Jager and G. Reijnen at a height ranging between 50-130 Kilometres. The rationale given my Oduntan is also similar. According to Gangale 'Neutralia' is in line

---

[171] *Supra* note 358 at 311
[172] *Id.*
[173] *Supra* Note 2
[174] Gangale, *Supra* Note 60, at 89

with some of the more reasonable theories that have been proposed. Firstly, it satisfies the aerodynamic lift theory. So as to ensure that a more capable aircraft is not in a position to become an exception the rule he chooses to increase the lower limit of the region (starting at 88.5 Kilometres) to an altitude higher than the upper limit required for aerodynamic lift (40 Kilometres). The upper limit of Neutralia satisfies the lowest orbital flight theory. Since the lowest orbital flight theory contends that the beginning of space must be the minimum height required for a satellite to orbit the earth (144 Kilometres). Neutralia extends this height by another 16 Kilometres to 160 kilometres.

Here the observations of the World meteorological organization (WMO) may be noted. According to the WMO if space is understood as a region of space flight, then assuming the lowest perigee of an orbiting satellite to be at an altitude of 130km, this altitude would correspond to the thermosphere.[175] Adding to this, various phenomenon of space weather occurs in 'geospace' which includes the ionosphere and overlaps with the thermosphere. Furthermore, according to the WMO, the international meteorological vocabulary defines the upper

---

[175] UNCOPUOS, Definition and delimitation of outer space: views of States members and permanent observers of the Committee, U.N Doc. A/AC.105/1112/Add.2, 3, available at A/AC.105/1112/Add.2 - Definition and delimitation of outer space: views of Thailand, Turkey, WHO & WMO (unoosa.org) (last visited Apr 30, 2022).

atmosphere as the portion the atmosphere beginning from the upper limit of mesospace which corresponds to an altitude of 80 to 90 kilometres.[176] Additionally it also noted that there is no "precise top of the atmosphere."[177] From this is can be deduced that the region lying roughly between 80 to 130 kilometres is unique in the sense that it is not air space and neither is it outer space as we know it. It shares some elements from both regions. It, therefore, scientifically reinforces the delimitation of what may very well be considered as Neutralia or mesospace or a buffer zone. However, it must be noted that the WMO recommended that space be defined as "The unlimited part of the universe including the upper atmosphere and extending above the atmosphere." [178] This was adopted by the Organizations 'commission for basic systems'. This definition is not an antithesis of the idea of near space, rather, it may be considered as an all-encompassing term including within it both near space and outer space. Oduntan also is of the view that the altitude of the neutralia region allows for States to not feel 'suffocated' due to the low ceiling of outer space. This proves particularly useful since it addresses the apprehension of the States with respect to national sovereignty, national security and economic interests of the State.

---

[176] *Id.*
[177] *Supra* note 175.
[178] *Supra* Note 175.

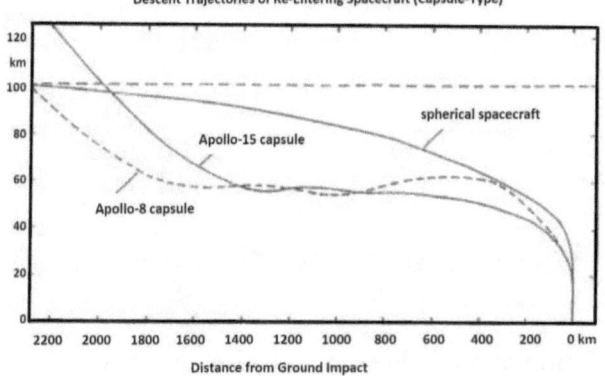

Figure 7: Re-entry trajectory of spacecrafts.[179]

---

[179] *Supra* Note 159, at 18

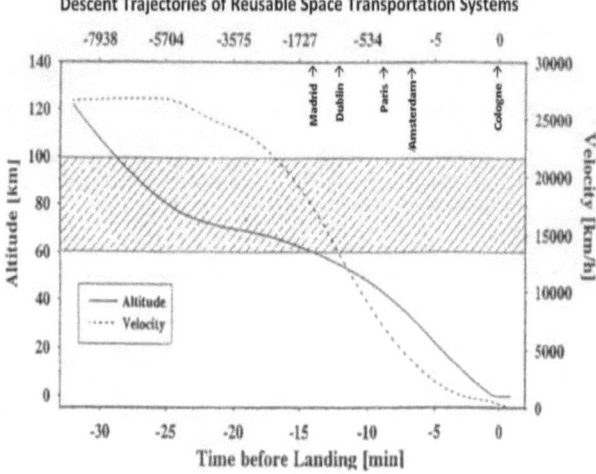

Figure 8: Re-entry trajectory of reusable spacecrafts.[180]

The above two illustrations also emphasise on the role that the buffer zone would play in the entry and decent of space vehicles. As is evident, space vehicles spend a considerable amount of time, over 30 minutes in and around the buffer zone at immensely high velocities. These velocities are considerably high even as they approach air space within which commercial airlines function. Furthermore, these images again point out to the vast distances these objects are covering in the horizontal plane at nearly all altitudes due to their high velocities. The importance of a buffer zone or Neutralia and the

---

[180] *Supra* Note 159, at 19

urgency for the same is quite evident. A perusal of the above illustrations, in light of the ever-growing air space and outer space traffic makes international cooperation within recognised frameworks not merely preferable but necessary.

It has also been noted that the establishment of a Neutralia recognizes the fact that a clean, that is to say, a precise delimitation of outer space is not a feasible prospect. The need for an intermediate zone becomes necessary to establish an element of relativity. [181] The emphasis on relativity becomes particularly important in aerospace travel and transportation since, as mentioned before, the high velocities and a relatively crowded air space and outer space can often mean that applicable legal regimes can change in a matter of milliseconds. The fact that the maritime domain has this element of relativity due to the establishment of Exclusive Economic Zones, Continental Shelves, territorial seas, and Internal waters among other things makes it something worth pondering over. Maritime regulations do not need to account for the same high speeds found in aerospace and yet knowingly or unknowingly -most likely the former- feature a gradual transformation from national sovereignty to the commons, or *res communis*.

---

[181] Proceedings Of the Space Law Conference 2006 Asian Cooperation in Space Activities a Common Approach to Legal Matters, 23, (2022). Available at: Microsoft Word - Thailand Conference Proceedings-revised 2.doc (mcgill.ca) (last visited May 1, 2022).

Thomas Gangale while writing on the matter of sovereignty in international aerospace goes to the extent of applying provisions of the UNCLOS *mutatis mutandis*. On the question of the right of 'hot pursuit', Gangale is of the view that while it may not be as simplistic as its application is in the maritime domain, it may very well be applicable. In light of the fact that no treaty on space law mentions it, he opines that Article 111 of the UNCLOS which concerns itself with the right of hot pursuit should be applicable. He states that like in the maritime domain the right of hot pursuit in the buffer zone shall be applicable as it would be international air space.

Magna Carta of Space

Having considered the various aspects of maritime law that can be adopted into space law the most obvious consideration that would now arise is the need to codify this framework including the established provisions of the existing outer space treaties, preferably into one international convention.

Fortunately, these efforts have been made by what has been referred to as the 'Magna Carta of Space'. On February 3rd, 1961 the Inter-America association at Bogota adopted the Magna Carta of Space (MCS). The Magna Carta of Space dealt with aspects of outer space that had been wilfully or not, left out of the five conventions on outer space. It is important to note that the magna carta of space was adopted before the five conventions were adopted. The magna carta of space among other things laid emphasis on the distinction on *'res communis'* and *'terra nullius'*[182] while considering outer space and the interplanetary system as *res communis*.[183] Importantly, while the magna carta of space recommended the division of space into Air

---

[182] Magna Carta of Space, Art 5. Available at: Microsoft Word - International Space Law Library 7-1.doc (ops-alaska.com) (last visited May 1, 2022).
[183] *Supra* Note 182, Art. 3,4

Space and Outer space [184] it recognised the impossibility of establishing a physical boundary having characteristics posed by those on land and at sea. It consequently proposes the establishment of 'neutral zone' that includes within it the upper limits of air space and the lower limit of outer space.[185] The magna carta of space Article 8 of which continues to state the rights and duties associated with this region referred to as 'Neutralia'. Among the rights and duties applicable to this region are:

a) "The right of innocent passage,
b) The duty not to attack or destroy a vehicle or object passing in this region,
c) The duty not to attack the nation from which the said vehicle or object was launched,
d) The duty not to destroy the occupants of the said vehicles or object,

without prior, sufficient warning and notice of claim of invasion of sovereignty and without prior opportunity for determination of the merits of such complaints by peaceful methods."[186]

The MCS also states that were such injury, death or damage to property is caused the then the state responsible for such injury, death or damage would be

---

[184] *Supra* Note 182, Art. 1
[185] *Supra* Note 182, Art. 8
[186] *Id.*

liable without the need to provide "proof of fault negligence, carelessness or recklessness."[187]

It also takes into consideration the safety of the airspace and states that subsequent provisions shall be made to prevent 'interference' with aircrafts by space vehicles, and between space vehicles.[188] Hence, even in 1961 despite a sparsely crowded air space and outer space the drafters of the MCS realised the importance of ensuring safety of not just outer space but air space too. Ideally it is not hard to imagine that on implementation of the treaty the ICAO would cooperate or even *de jure* adopted the role of a regulator of airspace even with respect to matters allied to outer space.

These ideas to regulate outer space and the foresight displayed by the MCS is remarkable. It is especially so, considering that the treaty was adopted only four years after the launch of sputnik and was six years ahead of the adoption of the outer space treaty. It is also remarkable for the fact that it addresses many of the issues that were raised much later at the UNCOPOUS and have yet remained unaddressed. Another interesting aspect of the Magna Carta of Space is that it seeks to create synergy between the various bodies which have a stake in the regulation of outer space affairs. It implicitly not only involves the ICAO by invoking the security of Air Space but also implicitly involves the ITU by covering with its ambit

---

[187] *Supra* Note 182, Art. 13
[188] *Supra* Note 182, Art. 12

the allocation and control of radio frequencies.[189] More importantly with respect to the matter in question the MCS largely ticks most of the boxes one would expect for an adequate means of delimitation of air space and outer space.

Perhaps among the few disappointments with the magna Carta was the lack of a precise delimitations for Neutralia. This omission can be attributed to the fact a precise delimitation would of course be the subject of debate and discussion and that the larger framework should not be delayed on account of that. The magna carta of space does, however, make reference to the altitudes where the general delimitation must of course commence and end.

---

[189] *Supra* Note 182, Art. 11

Suggested methodology of delimitation

A perusal of viable methods of delimitation makes it patently clear that all methodologies have short comings. It goes without saying that a perfect solution may never exist and would require the unanimous cooperation, acceptance, and necessary modification of international law if it were to ever exist. However, this is not to say that a most desirable solution may not exist or be adopted purely due to a few shortcomings.

A pluri-zonal delimitation of aerospace must be undertaken. This concept is not alien. Scholars, including Hyman, Oduntan, C. de Jager and G. Reijnen, and the Inter-American Bar Association have suggested it. This region has been referred to by many names such as Neutralia, Buffer Zone, Near Space and Transitionary Outer Space Zone (TOSZ) [190] among other names.

The first zone extending to a distance of 100 kilometres would be the extent of national airspace and of all rights associated with territorial sovereignty.

---

[190] *Supra* note 64, at 728

Ideally the height should be about 80 to 90 kilometres for the following reasons:

a)   Distances suggested by various scholars, including von Karman (83.3 kilometres) lies in the range of 80 to 90 kilometres barring a few exceptions.

b)   At this altitude it is nearly impossible for any object relying on aerodynamic lift or buoyancy to attain flight.

c)   An object that has attained this height can consequently be identified as one that mostly likely seeks to enter into sub orbital flight or orbital flight.

However, a height of 100 kilometres is preferable for the following reasons:

a)   It has been seen as an easier number to remember and also a round number.[191]

b)   It is flexible as it factors in the possible technological progress that can make aviation possible in the upper atmosphere.

c)   It has *de facto* acceptance from some States as the starting point of space as it is often difficult to maintain effective control at that distance.

d)   Adding another 10 to 20 Kilometres between the surface and the buffer zone would make States feel less suffocated.

e)   It is not contrary to the laws of most states which define the limits of their domestic airspace.

---

[191] *Supra* note 64, at 725

The second zone, hereafter referred to as Near space, would extend from 100 kilometres to 200 kilometres. This zone would be considered to be international aerospace. This region would be governed by both the ICAO and by any future organization formed for the regulation of outer space. Hence, the regulations of the ICAO, conventions dealing with air space, and conventions dealing with outer space shall be applicable to this region. Ideally, there should be one convention which will include all relevant factors within its purview. The rationale for this region may be listed as the following:

a) Would allow for the special regulation of sub-orbital flights, very low earth orbit satellites, High-altitude pseudo-satellites and High-Altitude platform stations among other things.

b) It would allow for the special regulation of any aircraft or any object that makes use of aerodynamic lift that may in the future be able to reach that distance.

c) It would allow for the creation of a separate regime for objects traversing through this region. This would include weapons (Including Intercontinental Ballistic Missiles), sounding rockets, space vehicles, and space objects entering into orbit.

d) It will foster synergy and cooperation of the international community in keeping both the air space and outer space safe by involving all relevant stake holders. This will include the ICAO, the UNCOPOUS, the ITU, and the international community at large.

e) It would reduce disputes while identifying the scientific point of delimitation of outer space while concomitantly allowing for a legal fiction to regulate space activities in what scientifically may not be considered as outer space. As mentioned previously, even at a distance of 130 Kilometres the phenomenon of space weather may be found. Furthermore the Earth's atmosphere extends for hundreds of kilometres beyond the surface of the earth, especially the Exosphere.

f) Considering the high velocities involved an immediate transference to a separate legal regime would lead to disputes especially when the act in question was committed near or in the proximity of either zone. A buffer zone would minimize disputes on account of a sui generis legal regime.

The region beyond a distance of 200 Kilometres will be outer space. It shall be regulated only be the five conventions of outer space and shall be based upon the spatial delimitation of outer space. The need for a spatial delimitation is justified due to the ease of application of a legal regime, the objectivity it provides in the determination of regions, and the wider general application it permits.

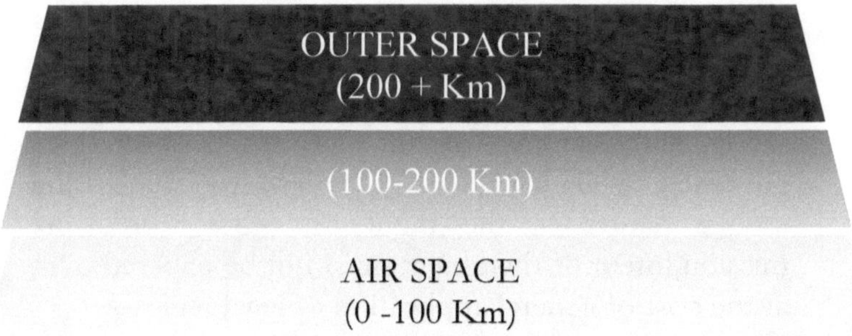

> **OUTER SPACE**
> **(200 + Km)**

> **(100-200 Km)**

AIR SPACE
(0 -100 Km)

Figure 9: Proposed delimitation of Air Space and Outer Space

Nevertheless, this must be blended with a functionalist approach. Amongst the foundational pillars of space law are the Liability convention and the Registration convention. Both these conventions are functionalist in their approach as they are applicable regardless of the position of the space object or space vehicle. This should not be seen as an exception to the general rule but rather a one aspect of a hybrid framework. The functionalist approach also becomes applicable when an object enters space. Since space is effectively an international common, territorial sovereignty can only be applicable within the confines of the space craft. The nature of laws applicable, depending upon the domestic legislation of the State and the mission of the spacecraft would vary. Therefore, a functionalist approach would be applicable in determining the laws applicable on and within the craft even as it crosses spatialist boundaries.

Furthermore, it would be necessary to moderate the spatialist application of laws by functionalist rationality. This is particularly the case where objects travelling into orbit or sub-orbits have to pass through air space. The legal regime applicable to safety and security of the air space should be governed by air laws, and space laws too due to the unique nature of the flight. In other words the mission intent of the object must not be papered over at the cost of general application of legal regimes.

This methodology largely addresses the various challenges faced by the international community. It stands in as a satisfactory methodology as it also addresses the fears of States with respect to national sovereignty, national security, and safety of the airspace and outer space among other things.

This methodology firstly, adheres to a minimum standard of scientific and technical checks. It factors into consideration scientific criteria pertaining to the regions in question. The requirement of aerodynamic lift for sustained flight remains a prominent consideration. The regions very nature has been factored in since it does not ignore the type of activities that occur in this region and even takes note of the very composition of the atmosphere in the respective regions. It is hence a solution that can either adapt to technological changes without altering its form or be sound enough to exist regardless of technological evolution.

Next, it covers all kinds of vehicles including those that traverse through air space only to enter sub orbital flights. Despite being a spatialist method of delimitation it does not ignore the 'mission intent' or in other words the *raison d'etre* of the flight. It is a rationale consideration that cannot and must not be ignored. This allows for specific and general application of laws concomitantly.

This methodology recognizes the ICAO, UNCOPOUS and the ITU among other bodies as stake holders. Hence, it promotes cooperation in both air space and outer space but most prominently in near space. Consequently, this leads to greater safety and coordination among stake holders. This methodology also provides a sufficient ceiling for territorial airspace so as to allow modern contemporary and future technologies to secure the safety of the State. National security must obviously be tempered by rationality and practical limitations. Within these constraints it is feasible that a ceiling of 100 Kilometers or more depending upon on the regulations applied to near space, is sufficient.

This methodology as mentioned previously also has precedent. The delimitation of the seas is quintessential precedent of regulating the commons by plurizonal delimitation. In both regions similar concerns crop up and hence maritime delimitation serves as an adequate precedent. Scholars have also proposed the idea of a plurizonal delimitation. Importantly such a delimitation prevents abrupt delimitations so as to avoid complex spatial issues.

Furthermore, this methodology does not involve any proposal that may very well be considered as unreasonable or extra ordinary. Often proposals in the past have been unfeasible or outright absurd, for instance the *ad infinitum* theory.

Seeking Delimitation

Even as we take our next step to become an interplanetary species, we are still struggling to delineate the boundaries, fictional or otherwise, of our home planet. From a civilizational perspective, the failure to do so typifies the lack of entente we have fostered amongst ourselves as we seek to compete for what we as a species ironically called 'the common heritage of mankind'.

The sea and space are no exceptions to this. Even as we compete for the resources they offer; one cannot help but notice the difference between both regimes. One hand the seas are regulated, for the most part, despite the dependence of large populations on the seas for food, commerce and livelihood. On the other hand outer space is the extra territorial equivalent of the wild west. The region between outer space and airspace, that is near space, epitomizes this especially. This leads us to answer the question of whether the delimitation of outer space and airspace would serve to bring about greater regulation of both air space and outer space. If this is answered in the affirmative, the legal regime applied to the seas can be successfully reproduced to the exigencies of outer space.

We can conclude that the limits of national sovereignty in the vertical sphere are not defined. However, this in no way implies that national sovereignty is unlimited. There is consensus on the fact that national sovereignty must end at outer space since the latter has been accorded the status of *Res communis*. It is also a scientific fact that outer space begins at a certain distance. Therefore both air space and national sovereignty must terminate at a set point. However, they need not be co-terminus. Air space and sovereignty can exist independent of the other. Sovereignty is a legal fiction and can be extended *ad infinitum* by mutual agreement. Furthermore, delimitation may also be pluri-zonal or non-binary. Regions apart from air space and outer space can and perhaps, should exist. Sovereignty can hence be extended beyond air space and yet, not into outer space.

Delimitation is also necessitated by the apparent conflict between air space and outer space. The very nature of the legal regimes applicable in both regions are for the most part in contrast to each other. This is so for obvious reasons. While on one hand the legal regime of airspace is determined by the sovereign territorial rights of states coupled with the physics of air space, outer space is a 'common', free from exercise of territorial sovereignty and subject to the peculiar characteristics of outer space. Both regions also differ due to their functionality in terms of commerce, defence and exploration. Furthermore, while airspace has its very own regulatory body - the ICAO - outer space continues to be at the mercy of states cooperating out of necessity and a hint of good will. Delimitation, either bi-zonal or pluri-zonal, of outer space will only make these difference more apparent.

The adoption of such a regime would truly be revolutionary and would likely transform into customary international law. The nature of the methodology is such that it is likely to be flexible enough to accommodate evolving technologies and scientific development while concomitantly ensuring that delimitation of outer space evolves with time and keeps up with technological progress. It will positively affect the safety of aerospace. This includes not just air space but the entirety of space, both near and outer.

An analysis of municipal law also makes it obvious that by and large, States have not necessarily taken a contrarian position to what has been proposed in this book. Barring a few exceptions, States have implicitly and explicitly acknowledged the limits of their territorial sovereignty. Some States like Mexico have acknowledged that the limit of its territorial sovereignty depends very much on the rules established by international law. The interests of states largely pertaining to national security must and have been considered.

It is also important to note that certain methods of delimitations which by their very nature are unilateral in their origin must be relegated to academic history. One such example would be the Astronaut Badge Line. It is the limit beyond which any person crossing it is considered an Astronaut by NASA. The rationale is that such a unilateral methodology of delimitation will appear as the application of soft power and hegemony of a States in influencing the law-making process of the international community. International law in the 21st century must be a product of a healthy discourse free from diplomatic influences and subject only to legal, practical and scientific considerations. Delimitation by judicial settlement is a legal operation which must be based "on considerations of law". In this respect, it has to be mentioned, as confirmed by jurisprudence, that there is a distinction between delimitation based on legal rules and delimitation by States during negotiations, which involves political considerations, among others.[192]

While it is a fact of Westphalian diplomacy that States seek to influence the rules and norms of international law, the challenges that face us in the 21st century require a bipartisan approach especially when matters concerning the common heritage of mankind are in question. Solutions offered must be such that they avoid the tragedy of the commons. The stark contrast between developed and other States is largely apparent in the positions they have adopted. While developed nations do not see the urgency in delimitation of outer space, developing states see the urgency in the matter. This has primarily been so since the inability to actively explore space would in

---

[192] Handbook on the Delimitation of Maritime Boundaries, 18 (2000).

the future translate into dilution of their stakes in determining the future of aerospace and outer space.

The thought and sight of outer space can very often put our lives into perspective; it reminds us of our very own mortality, our miniscule footprint on the timescale, our isolation and perhaps even our cosmical insignificance. Yet in space, in this randomised chaos, the human spirit remains undeterred. We constantly seek to define, organize, classify, debate and delineate, the environment around us. In fact, as a species this is our distinguishing trait. Space is no exception to this. As we become an interplanetary species one hopes that these traits will allow us to bring order to the periphery of our Planet.

Bibliography

PRIMARY SOURCES

UN REPORTS/DOCUMENTS

a) Addendum to the Draft Report of Committee on the Peaceful Uses of Outer Space, *in* United Nations General Assembly para 31 (2015), https://www.unoosa.org/pdf/limited/c2/AC105_C2_L296Add01E.pdf (last visited Apr 18, 2022)

b) Addendum to the Draft Report of Committee on the Peaceful Uses of Outer Space, *in* United Nations General Assembly para 31 (2015), https://www.unoosa.org/pdf/limited/c2/AC105_C2_L296Add01E.pdf (last visited Apr 18, 2022)

c) UNCOPUOS, Draft report, U.N Doc. A/AC.105/C.2/L.296/Add.1, 5, available at Microsoft Word - fb25d410-4551-43fe-8305-ccc82316b0d9_in_for_PDF_printing.doc (unoosa.org) (last visited Apr 30, 2022)

d) UNCOPUOS, Draft report, U.N Doc. A/AC.105/C.2/L.296/Add.1, 5, available at Microsoft Word - fb25d410-4551-43fe-8305-ccc82316b0d9_in_for_PDF_printing.doc (unoosa.org) (last visited Apr 30, 2022)

e) UNCOPUOS, Draft report, U.N Doc. A/AC.105/C.2/L.321/Add.2

f) UNCOPUOS, *National legislation and practice relating to the definition and delimitation of outer space,* ,2, U.N Doc A/AC.105/865/Add.23, (January 20, 2020)

g) UNCOPUOS, *National legislation and practice relating to the definition and delimitation of outer space,* ,1, A/AC.105/865/Add.19, (January 20, 2020)

h) UNCOPUOS, *National legislation and practice relating to the definition and delimitation of outer space,* A/AC.105/865/Add.4, (February 9, 2009)

i) UNCOPUOS, Questionnaire on Possible Legal Issues with Regard to Aerospace Objects: Replies from Member States, U.N Doc. A/AC.105/635/Add.15, 4-5, available at: A AC.105 635 Add.3-EN.pdf (last visited Apr 30, 2022).

j) UNCOPUOS, Questionnaire on Possible Legal Issues with Regard to Aerospace Objects: Replies from Member States, U.N Doc. A/AC.105/635/Add.14, 5, available at: Microsoft Word - V0780807.doc (unoosa.org) (last visited Apr 30, 2022).

k) UNCOPUOS, Questionnaire on possible legal issues with regard to aerospace objects: replies from Member States, U.N Doc. A/AC.105/635/Add.15, 3, available at untitled (unoosa.org) (last visited Apr 30, 2022).

l) UNCOPUOS, Questionnaire on Possible Legal Issues with Regard to Aerospace Objects:

Replies from member States, U.N Doc. A/AC.105/635/Add.3, 4, available at A/AC.105/635/ Add.3 (unoosa.org) (last visited Apr 30, 2022).

m) UNCOPUOS, The Question of The Definition And/Of the Delimitation of Outer Space, U.N Doc. A_AC-105_C-2_7_Add-1, 8, available at https://digitallibrary.un.org/record/741816?ln=en (last visited Apr 30, 2022).

n) UNOOSA Press Release, *The Definition and Delimitation of Outer Space: The Present Need to Determine Where "Space Activities" Begin*, available at https://www.unoosa.org/pdf/pres/lsc2014/tech-04E.pdf

ICAO REPORTS/DOCUMENTS

a) Airspace Sovereignty, *in* Worldwide Air Transport Conference (ATCONF) 2 (2022), http://www.icao.int/meetings/atconf6

b) International Civil Aviation Organization (ICAO), *Convention on Civil Aviation ("Chicago Convention")*, 7 December 1944, (1994) 15 U.N.T.S. 295

c) International Civil Aviation Organization Secretariat, *Operations Above Flight Level 600*, 2 (ICAO Working Paper AN-Conf/13-WP/16 12/6/18), https://www.icao.int/Meetings/anconf13/Documents/WP/wp_016_en.pdf, last accessed on 24-11-2020

d) International Civil Aviation Organization, *Commercial Space Flights,* (ICAO, Working Paper LC/36-WP/3-2 20/10/15)

e) International Institute if Space Law, *The 40th Colloquium on the Law of Outer Space Turin, Italy*

f) International Civil Aviation Organization, Resolutions Adopted by The Assembly and Index to Documentation 71, 72 (1992), available at: https://www.icao.int/assembly-archive/Session29/A.29.RESOL.9600.EN.pdf (last visited May 1, 2022).

g) Commercial Space Flights, LC/36-WP/3-2, *in* Legal Committee – 36th Session, 5, (2015), available at: https://www.icao.int/Meetings/LC36/Working%20Papers/LC%2036%20-%20WP%203-2.en.pdf (last visited May 1, 2022).

CONVENTIONS/TREATIES

a) Agreement on the Rescue of Astronauts, the Return of Astronauts and the Return of Objects Launched into Outer Space, Dec *19 1967, 610 UNTS 205*

b) Convention on registration of objects launched into outer space, Sep 15, 1976, 1023 UNTS 15

c) Convention Relating to the Regulation of Aerial Navigation, opened for signature Oct. 13, 1919, 11 L.N.T.S. 173.

d) International Civil Aviation Organization (ICAO), *Convention on Civil Aviation ("Chicago Convention")*, 7 December 1944, (1994) 15 U.N.T.S. 295

e) International Civil Aviation Organization (ICAO), *Convention on Civil Aviation ("Chicago Convention")*, 7 December 1944, (1994) 15 U.N.T.S. 295

f) Magna Carta of Space, 3 February 1961

g) The 1976 Declaration of the First Meeting of Equatorial Countries, Dec 3, 1976

h) Treaty on Principles Governing the activities of States in the exploration and Use of Outer Space, including the Moon and Other Celestial Bodies, 19 December 1966, 610 U.N.T.S. 205

i) United Nations Convention on the Law of the Sea, Dec. 2, 1982, 1833 U.N.T.S.397

STATUTES

a) Austrian Aviation Rules were revised in 2014 (see Austrian Federal Law Gazette II No. 297/2014)

b) Outer Space and High-altitude Activities Act (New Zealand), No. 209 of 2017, 4 (2017).

CASES

a) *Bury V. Pope* [1587] Bro Eliz 118.
b) Continental Shelf (*Libya v. Malta*), 1985 I.C.J. 13
c) Legal Status of Eastern Greenland. (Norway V. Denmark). Permanent Court of International Justice, 1933. [1933] P.C.I.J
d) *Nicaragua v. United States of America* 986 I.C.J. 14
e) *Reinhardt v. Newport Flying Service Corp.*, 133 N.E. 371 (NY, 1921).

SECONDARY SOURCES

BOOKS

a) Black's Law Dictionary, (9th ed. 2009).
b) Gbenga Oduntan, *Sovereignty and Jurisdiction In Airspace And Outer Space,* (Routledge 2012)
c) Hermann Heller & David Dyzenhaus, *Sovereignty: A Contribution to the Theory of Public and International Law,* (Oxford Scholarship Online 2019)
d) Space Safety Regulations and Standards, 246 (Joseph Pelton & Ram Jakhu 1 ed. 2010).

e) Thomas Gangale, *how high is the sky? The Definition and Delimitation of Outer Space and Territorial Airspace in International Law*, (Brill Nijhoff, 2018)

JOURNALS

a) Abdurrasyid Dr. H. Priya, *State Sovereignty in Airspace*, 6 Neliti 487 (2009

b) Alex. S. Li, *Ruling Outer Space: Defining the Boundary and Determining Jurisdictional Authority*, Oklahoma law Review.

c) Conor McGlynn, *Aristotle's Economic Defence of Private Property*, XXIX The Student Economic Review 2

d) Dean N. Reinhardt, *The Vertical Limit of State Sovereignty*, 72 Journal of Air Law and Commerce 70 (2007), available at: https://scholar.smu.edu/cgi/viewcontent.cgi?article=1126&context=jalc (last visited Apr 18, 2022).

e) Frans G Von Dunk., *THE DELIMITATION OF OUTER SPACE REVISITED The Role of National Space Laws in the Delimitation Issue.* 51, University of Nebraska, Space, Cyber, and Telecommunications Law Program (1998)

f) Garrett Hardin, *The Tragedy of the Commons: The population problem has no technical solution; it requires a fundamental extension in morality.*, 162 Science (1968),

g) Gbenga Oduntan, *The Never Ending Dispute: Legal Theories on the Spatial Demarcation Boundary Plane between Airspace and Outer Space*, 1 Hertfordshire Law Journal 64, 81 (2003), http://www.herts.ac.uk/fms/documents/schools/law/HLJ_V1I2_Oduntan.pdf (last visited May 4, 2022).

h) Jonathan C. McDowell, *The edge of space: Revisiting the Karman Line*, 151 Acta Astronautica (2018).

i) Lora D. Lashbrook, *Ad Coelum Maxim As Applied to Aviation Law*, 21 Notre Dame L. Rev. (1946).

j) Lubos Perek, *Scientific Criteria for the Delimitation of Outer Space*, 5 J. Space L. 111 (1977).

k) Paul Dempsey & Maria Manoli, *Suborbital Flights and the Delimitation of Airspace Vis-à-Vis Outer Space: Functionalism, Spatialism and State Sovereignty*, 42 Annals of Air and Space Law 222 (2017).

l) Rhys Monahan, *The sky's the limit? Establishing a legal delimitation of airspace and outer space* 32, 2008

m) Sarah Louise Vollmer, *The Right Stuff in Geospace: Using Mutual Coercion to Avoid an Inevitable Prison for Humanity*, 51 St. Mary's Law Journal 787

INTERNET SOURCES

a) Bas Bolman et al., Oceans Report - Addressing SDG14 issues with factual data and state of the art knowledge. 8 (2022), available at: https://www.researchgate.net/publication/331928317_Oceans_Report_-_Addressing_SDG14_issues_with_factual_data_and_state_of_the_art_knowledge (last visited May 1, 2022).

b) Brian Dunbar, Earth's Atmospheric Layers NASA (2013), https://www.nasa.gov/mission_pages/sunearth/science/atmosphere-layers2.html (last visited Apr 13, 2022).

c) Gbenga Oduntan, Air Law & Space Law: spatial delimitation between airspace & outer space (2016), https://www.youtube.com/watch?v=QQbHvIj9isA (last visited Apr 18, 2022).

d) Proceedings Of the Space Law Conference 2006 Asian Cooperation in Space Activities a Common Approach to Legal Matters, 23, (2022). Available at: [Microsoft Word - Thailand Conference Proceedings-revised 2.doc (mcgill.ca)](#) (last visited May 1, 2022).

e) Statement about the Karman Line, World Air Sports Federation (2018), https://www.fai.org/news/statement-about-karman-line (last visited May 4, 2022).

f) The Quest for a Legal Frontier between Airspace and Outer Space, *in* Space Law Webinar #2 (2020), https://iaass.space-safety.org/events/courses/space-law-webinar-2-the-quest-for-a-legal-frontier-between-airspace-and-outer-space/ (last visited Apr 18, 2022).

NEWS SOURCES

a) Danielle Ireland-Piper, NASA is facing its first space crime — so, what happens if you commit a crime in space? The Print (2019), https://theprint.in/science/nasa-is-facing-its-first-space-crime-so-what-happens-if-you-commit-a-crime-in-space/284410/ (last visited Apr 13, 2022).

b) Gerry Hadden, Palomares bombs: Spain waits for US to finish nuclear clean-up BBC News (2012), https://www.bbc.com/news/magazine-18689132 (last visited Apr 30, 2022).

c) The New Indian Express, *NASA astronaut Anne McClain says she did not hack her spouse's data*, 2019, https://www.newindianexpress.com/world/2019/aug/25/nasa-astronaut-anne-mcclain-says-she-did-not-hack-her-spouses-data-2024085.html (last visited Apr 13, 2022).

About the Author

Noel Jackson

Noel is an Advocate, public policy professional, and a former LAMP fellow. After graduating from law School he pursued a Master's degree in Space and Telecommunication laws from NALSAR, Hyderabad. He manages 'Space Law Decluttered', a blog dedicated to coalescing views on space law and policy. Cheesecake is his manna, filter coffee his elixir and gardening his passion.

www.ingramcontent.com/pod-product-compliance
Lightning Source LLC
LaVergne TN
LVHW041950070526
838199LV00051BA/2972